MW00682961

Rooftop Kids

Carol Reinsma

Devotional Stories for LiFE

CRC Publications
Grand Rapids, Michigan

The Scripture quotations in this publication are from the
HOLY BIBLE, NEW INTERNATIONAL READER'S
VERSION, © 1994, 1996 International Bible Society. Used by
permission of Zondervan Bible Publishers. All rights
reserved.

Rooftop Kids: Devotional Stories for LiFE. © 1999, CRC
Publications, 2850 Kalamazoo Ave. SE, Grand Rapids,
MI 49560.

All rights reserved. With the exception of brief excerpts for
review purposes, no part of this book may be reproduced in
any manner whatsoever without written permission from
the publisher. Printed in the United States of America on
recycled paper. ✪

We welcome your comments. Call 1-800-333-8300 or e-mail
us at editors@crcpublications.org.

ISBN 1-56212-407-2

Library of Congress Cataloging in Publication Data
L of C info here.

10 9 8 7 6 5 4 3 2 1

In writing from the imaginary rooftops of homes long ago, I looked at the picture of God given to us in the Bible.

Three thousand years ago God was holy, powerful, and merciful—a God who desired the hearts of people. Today God is the same. It is an exciting journey to see who God was, is, and will be.

I want to thank those who helped me during this writing process.

My husband, Jerry, who encouraged me to visit Israel at the beginning of this project so I could see and experience the land. And because he is my faithful friend and supporter.

George and Fran Kroeze, Helen DeJong, and all the others who were my fellow travelers to Israel.

Teri Downs and Sherrill Larson for their anointing prayers.

Mary Bahr Fritts, Mary Peace Finley, and Barb Reinhard for their suggestions and critiques.

Soshanna and Micah Harrari for their guidance in understanding biblical harps.

And to my Lord and Savior, to whom belongs all honor and praise.

Carol Reinsma

Contents

Preface

Dear Family:

Welcome to the rooftop of an Israelite house. The rooftop was an important part of the home in biblical days. It was a place to work, pray, and play. The Israelite homes were either large two-story houses where related families lived together, or small mud-brick or stone houses.

These fictional stories take place over three different time periods. The first group happens in Bethel when Samuel was a young boy in the temple at Shiloh. The second group takes place in Mizpah just before the time Samuel called the people of Israel back to God. And the last section takes place during the time King David moved his palace to Jerusalem.

Each week begins with a tie-in to the Bible story from Year 2 for grades 1 and 2 of the LiFE church school curriculum. Perhaps your first- or second-grade child could help you decide when to use these devotions. If you decide to use them with the whole family, your first or second grader could take charge of opening the book, dividing up the parts for the echo reading, finding the Bible passage and the song for the week, and telling the rest of the family the Bible story at the beginning of the week. If you decide to use the book as bedtime devotions, you'll find what you need to have a special story and discussion time with your child. The time you spend together may also help establish a personal evening devotional time for your child later in life.

If your child misses a lesson or if none of your children are first- or second-grade LiFE students, read the suggested Bible story from the Scripture for the week (we suggest using the New International Reader's Version of the Bible) and then, during the rest of the week, enjoy the five *Rooftop* stories.

The introduction to each week includes an echo reading, a song for the week (from *Songs for LiFE,* a children's hymnal published with the LiFE curriculum), and a prayer. The echo reading, the song, and the prayer are meant to be used all week long. Each daily story is introduced by a Scripture verse from the New International Reader's Version. Your child may want to mark these verses with a colored pencil in his or her Bible so that later you can see which verses you have read. Each day's story is followed by one or two "I Wonder" statements. Wonder together about these statements and about other things that may be happening in your lives.

At Christmastime and Easter time your child's church school curriculum includes stories for these celebrations. There are no *Rooftop* stories for these weeks. Take this time with your family to explore special devotional material related to these important times in the church year. As you read together these fictional stories of people who lived nearly three thousand years before you, may you gain a clearer sense of what it was like to live so long ago. And may you also know that God has always been with his people, has always had the power, has always known all things—and will continue to do so.

Carol Reinsma

Echo Praises

When Joshua brought the people into the promised land, he had half of the people stand on one mountain (Mount Gerizim) and the other half stand on the opposite mountain (Mount Ebal). The people recited the law and the blessings across from each other (Josh. 8:30-35).

In the hills of Ephraim it is believed that the people climbed certain hills that stood across from each other and echoed back and forth praises to God. And when David was king, musicians sang and shouted praises in the streets when worshiping the Lord.

In this book, the praises are called Echo Praises. If you have just two people, you can echo the praises back and forth to each other. If you have more people, divide into two groups. The ones on the first side are called Lambs. The ones on the opposite side are called Kids (baby goats).

You may not have two hills where you can stand across from each other, or a group to gather in the city streets, but you can shout and sing the praises with each other from across the table, across the room, or wherever you wish.

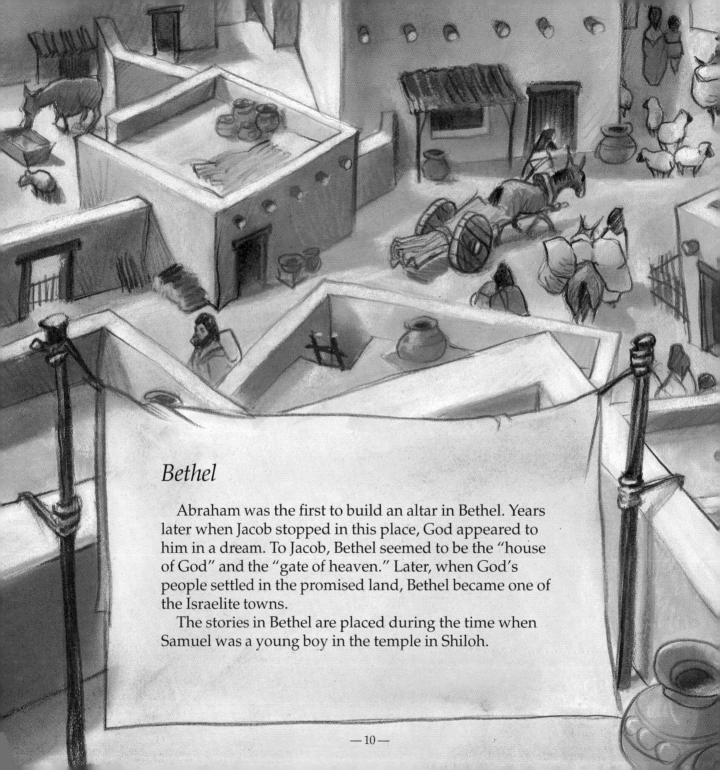

Bethel

Abraham was the first to build an altar in Bethel. Years later when Jacob stopped in this place, God appeared to him in a dream. To Jacob, Bethel seemed to be the "house of God" and the "gate of heaven." Later, when God's people settled in the promised land, Bethel became one of the Israelite towns.

The stories in Bethel are placed during the time when Samuel was a young boy in the temple in Shiloh.

Rooftop Kids of Bethel

Taavi (11)

He is the oldest child in the house and a strong worker in his father's fields. Because he knows he can do most things, he is proud. He wants the others to look up to him.

Sapphira (9)

Grandfather calls her his "little nutshell." She likes to run barefoot through the hills surrounding Bethel. Sapphira is a loyal friend with a loving and kind heart. Sometimes she does things secretly because she's afraid of what someone else might think.

Yerick (8)

He loves animals. The sheep and goats depend on him and trust him. He treats his friends with the same loving concern. When he is happy, he whistles. When he is sad, he talks to God while in the fields—or to his friends when they are around.

Kyla (11)

She loves beautiful things and likes to be admired for her own beauty. In order to be truly happy, Kyla needs to know and understand a different kind of beauty, one that comes from the inside.

Jensine (8)

She is quiet. She learns things by watching and listening. Even though she may not talk a lot about her feelings, she has a heart that is easily hurt and one that loves deeply. She loves to dance and celebrate God's goodness.

Chana (9)
She is a happy and bubbly person—a gift-giver who thinks of others and what they need.

Martha (6)
She is innocent and trusting. But she is easily frightened by thunder, lightning, and being left alone.

Joel (10)
He has a way of making everyone laugh and feel comfortable. Unlike his twin, Joosef, he is athletic. He likes adventure and spends most of his time roaming through the hills, looking for animals and hidden caves.

Joosef (10)
He is taller than his older twin, but one of his legs is shorter than the other. That means he limps and isn't as fast or as strong as Joel. He likes to stay close to home and help his parents or spend time with Grandfather.

Zuka (8)
He is a runaway slave. He comes to Bethel to get food and to hear more about God.

Animals

GOATS	SHEEP	DONKEYS/HORSES
Nusi	Noga	Nur
Muppem		Fifne
Ofer		
Phizibah		
Gillie		
Giza		
Zimra		
Anatie		

Creation: Skies, Seas, Plants, and Trees

Genesis 1:1-19

Praise God this week for light, water, and plants. Praise God with words from Psalm 104:1-2, 7-8, 13-14. Have one group or one person be the Lambs. The second group or person—the Kids (the baby goats)—echoes with the words on the right.

Litany	
Lambs	**Kids**
LORD, my God,	
	you are very great.
You are dressed in glory.	
	You are wrapped in robes of light.
You gave orders to the waters,	
	and they ran away.
They flowed down the mountains.	
	They went into the valleys
and made the rivers,	
	oceans, and lakes.
You make the grass grow	
	and plants for people to take care of.
The earth is filled—	
	filled with the things you have made.

Song for the Week
"Who Made Ocean, Earth, and Sky?" *Songs for LiFE* 91

Prayer for the Week
LORD, my God, you are very great.
I praise you for all you have made. Amen.

The Water Girl

Sapphira squeezed into the line formed by her brother and cousins. She held onto Jensine's tunic. And Chana grabbed onto Sapphira. In a minute her brother, Taavi, would start the game.

"Ready, set," called Taavi. Then he took off running, pulling this way and that.

"I can do it," Sapphira whispered to herself. "Yes, I can. I won't let go."

But then Taavi twisted with a sharp turn around the steps leading up to the rooftop of the house. Sapphira's arm scraped on the stone wall. And she let go. The line stopped.

Taavi marched up to Sapphira. "You lost. You let go."

"Sapphira lost," her twin cousins, Joosef and Joel, chanted.

"She's our water girl," said cousin Jensine.

Sapphira kicked a pebble with her bare toe. Why did she have to lose the game? She wanted to be in the olive groves today. It was the first day of picking olives, and everyone would be in a joyful mood. But not her. She would be running back and forth to the stream, filling the goatskin water bag and bringing it to the workers.

Her cousins and brother skipped off.

"What's the matter, my little nutshell?" Grandfather asked.

"I wish water were everywhere," Sapphira said. "Then I wouldn't have to carry it."

I Wonder . . .
I wonder if you know how Sapphira feels . . .

LORD, you have made so many things! How wise you were when you made all of them.

Psalm 104:24

A Riddle

"Hmm, water everywhere." Grandfather combed his fingers through his beard. "That reminds me of a riddle. What was full of water, but didn't hold water?"

Sapphira wrinkled her nose. "I don't get it."

"Think about it," Grandfather said. "If you can figure out the meaning, there'll be a special job for you. One that you'll enjoy."

Sapphira leaned her nut-brown head up against Grandfather's round middle. "Thanks, Grandfather. You make riddles exciting."

A goatskin pouch hung on the courtyard wall. Sapphira grabbed it and a copper cup too. She leaped over rocks on her way to the stream, wondering what was full of water but didn't hold water. Thump, slap. The goatskin water pouch bumped against her thighs. It was a strong water bag; not the kind that would have a hole. Not the kind that wouldn't hold water.

Up ahead the stream sparkled under the sunlight. Sapphira knew that the water tingled with coolness. A shadow darted across the stream. Quickly, she crouched behind a big rock.

A boy knelt beside the stream. He panted near the surface of the water.

Sapphira kept low while scooting closer to the boy under the cover of rock piles. Short bristles of hair stood up on his once-shaved head. Then, quick as a thirsty gazelle, he put his whole face into the stream, drinking the clear, clean water.

I Wonder . . .
I wonder when water seems like a gift to you . . .

You make springs pour water into the valleys.

Psalm 104:10a

A Cup of Water

Sapphira's fingers touched the smooth copper cup strapped to her waistband. It was easier to swallow water from a cup than it was to drink directly from the stream. Should she offer it to the boy?

She approached him, holding the cup in front of her. He jumped up when her shadow fell on the ground beside him. Dust and dirt outlined his wild-looking eyes. Gritty sand covered him from head to toe. This boy had to be thirstier than she had ever been.

Slowly, so as not to frighten him, Sapphira dipped the cup into the stream. Then she handed it to the boy. He drank without stopping.

As he gulped the water, she studied him. The once-shaved head told her that he wasn't an Israelite. Perhaps he came to Bethel to spy or cause trouble. She gripped her goatskin pouch.

With a smile on his cracked lips, he handed the cup back to her.

Sapphira relaxed. "My pouch holds more water," she said.

He nodded. But she wasn't sure if he understood.

"I'll fill it for you," she said and hopped onto a rock in the middle of the stream. She let the cool water pour into the goatskin pouch.

Then she handed it to him. He grabbed it and was gone—as quick as a fox.

I Wonder . . .

I wonder if you've ever done something kind for someone you didn't know . . .

If your enemy . . . is thirsty, give him water to drink.

Proverbs 25:21

Another Try

Sapphira watched bushes snap behind the boy. She should have told him that the water bag wasn't for keeps. But perhaps he would need it to stay alive.

Taavi and the others would be wondering by now where their water was. There wasn't time to fetch another goatskin and come back to the stream. Water from the well would just have to do. She could use the well bucket to carry the water.

When she got to the well, she lowered the bucket that was attached to a rope. Plop. The bucket splashed into the water. Tugging on the rope, she brought the bucket back up. The water was cool and dark. She tilted the bucket to take a drink. The stone coolness of the water tumbled down her throat. It was good, making her feel strong. She fussed with the knot on the rope. But it was an old knot, a knot that was tied by someone stronger than herself. She couldn't use the bucket to carry water.

Two brown birds with yellow bellies landed on the stone edge of the well. They eyed Sapphira as if she had something for them. "Okay," she said with a sigh. She poured the water into the animal watering hole beside the well. Without waiting for an invitation, the birds chirped and fluttered their wings in the water.

"I know how you feel," she said to them. "But there are a few others who want water too. And when I see Grandfather, I'm going to tell him that if something is full of water, there better be a way to hold and carry it too."

I Wonder . . .
I wonder if Sapphira wished she hadn't been so quick to help the thirsty stranger . . .

People of Israel,
he will save you.
That will bring
you joy like water
that is brought up
from wells.

Isaiah 12:3

Water from a Hidden Cave

The birds left the well. They soared into the hills, disappearing into a cave.

Grandfather had talked about a cave that had a deep spring. Once he had whispered to Sapphira about an old goatskin that he left up there to carry this special water. Without thinking about whether or not this was the right cave, she scrambled up the hill.

As she entered the cave, she reached along the walls of the cave. Surely goodness was with her. She found what she was hoping for—the silky sides of a goatskin.

Sapphira's fingers touched a wet trickle. She followed it. Now her eyes, used to the darkness, spied a pool of water. She scooped the precious liquid into the goatskin pouch.

When the pouch was full, she squirmed out of the cave's small opening. Then she ran as if the wind was behind her. "Cold water," she called as she neared the olive trees.

Soon she was surrounded by a thirsty brother and cousins.

"Magnificent water!" Taavi said, taking another gulp.

Sapphira thought about all the places she found water. "Grandfather, I know the answer to your riddle. Before God finished creating the world, water was everywhere, but there was no place to hold the water. Without the rivers and streams, we could never fill our water bags." Yes, Grandfather was right. She thought about giving water to the boy and the birds. And then she knew what else Grandfather had in mind. It was special being a water girl—almost fun.

I Wonder . . .
I wonder how many ways you can think of that we use the water God gives us . . .

The One who shows his tender love to them will guide them. Like a shepherd, he will lead them beside springs of water.

Isaiah 49:10b

Creation: Owls and Octopuses, Panthers and People

Genesis 1:20-2:3

God finished the creation. And it all worked together—the light, the land, the water, the plants, the fish, the birds, and the animals. It was just right for people. Praise God for the creation with words from Isaiah 45:18:

Litany	
Lambs	**Kids**
The LORD created the heavens.	
	He is God.
The LORD formed the earth and made it.	
	He set it firmly in place.
The LORD didn't create it to be empty.	
	He formed it for people to live on.
He says, "I am the LORD.	
	There is no other LORD."

Song for the Week
"For the Beauty of the Earth," *Songs for LiFE* 89

Prayer for the Week
Thank you, Lord, for showing us
that you are the Creator.
We praise you! Amen.

The Missing Goatskin

Give thanks to
the LORD.
Worship him.

Psalm 105:1a

Sapphira lifted up the old goatskin and poured water into the bread flour.

"Don't use that old bag," Taavi said. "Use the new one Grandmother made."

"I—I don't know where it is." That was the truth. She didn't know what happened to the boy or the goatskin.

"Well you'd better find it. If you don't, I'll tell Grandmother. And she'll probably take your goat, Nusi, and make a skin out of her."

Sapphira wrinkled her nose at Taavi. The small speckled goat that she had named Nusi was a gift from Grandfather. Sapphira would never let anything happen to that silky, wet-nosed nuzzler who gave such sweet milk.

"I'll find the bag," she said, "by sundown."

"You'd better," Taavi said. "At sundown we're going to the hills to welcome in the Feast of the Trumpets. Tomorrow we're going to Shiloh. We'll need a strong, large water bag for the trip."

The Feast of the Trumpets was Sapphira's favorite feast day. If it wasn't for Taavi giving her a hard time, she'd be leaping around like the playful Nusi. Celebrating creation and the new year made her feel new inside. Mother had made new clothes for the family too.

Sapphira buried her hands in the sticky dough. Could she find the boy and talk him into trading goatskins?

I Wonder . . .
I wonder what "celebrating creation" means . . .

A Fair Trade?

Sapphira slapped the dough. Her mother had told her to make six loaves. But with quick twists, Sapphira pinched the dough into seven pieces. The boy might be more willing to trade if there was a loaf of bread in the deal. Was it right to ask for the goatskin? Didn't she already have more than he did? All he had was one nice goatskin—one that she wanted back. If only there were more than a loaf of bread to offer him.

Sapphira carried the bread to the oven. Quickly she placed the loaves on the hot stones. The heat flowed over her as the grayish-white mounds of dough turned to a golden brown.

When Sapphira tapped one of the brown loaves, it sounded hollow. That meant the bread was done. She removed the hot loaves from the oven and carefully lined them up on cool stones. She wrapped the biggest loaf in the folds of her outer robe.

When no one was looking, Sapphira sidestepped out of the courtyard. Her big toe struck a rock. She limped with the pain, wishing toes wouldn't hurt so much. Then she ran down the hill of Bethel and toward the stream. As she crossed the valley, the dry grass prickled her feet.

She hurried to the well and looked back toward Bethel. No one had followed her. Soon she'd be at the stream and so would the boy. She hoped.

I Wonder...
I wonder if bread is a good gift for the stranger . . .

Tell the nations what the LORD has done.

Psalm 105:1b

—23—

A Spy

Sing to him. Sing praise to him. Tell about all of the wonderful things he has done.

Psalm 105:2

When Sapphira reached the stream, she heard the shrill whistle of a rock badger. It was fun to watch the little creatures cut down the dry grass and stack it into piles. Then she heard another whistle. That wasn't a badger's sound, was it?

Perhaps it was the boy, imitating the rock badgers. She had done that before.

What a good guess! Just beyond an almond tree, the boy sat on a rock. He was pulling up clumps of dried grass and piling them up for the rock badgers.

As sneaky as a fox, Sapphira approached him. She thought she could surprise him, but she didn't notice the dry twig in the path. She stepped right on it and watched the boy jump at the sound. His hand clamped down on the goatskin.

"It's me," she said. "I brought you bread."

"Sapphira," he whispered.

This time it was her turn to be surprised. "How do you know my name?"

"I've been watching you," he said. "And I know you worship the Hebrew God."

His answer caught her off guard. Sapphira stared at him, wondering what he really wanted. But she wasn't afraid of him. Instead, he made her think of their donkey, Fifne. Grandfather brought Fifne home after rescuing her from a man who beat his animals with a stick.

I Wonder . . .
I wonder how the boy knew that Sapphira worshiped God . . .
I wonder if other people know that you worship God . . .

Zuka

Sapphira pointed to the goatskin. "My brother wants our water bag."

"I noticed Taavi likes to be in charge," the boy said, handing her the bag.

He grabbed the bread she held toward him. Hungrily, he tore the bread apart and stuffed it into his mouth.

"What else do you know?" she asked.

"You live in Bethel with your family. And your cousins, Kyla, Jensine, Chana, Martha, and Yerick. And sometimes your other cousins, Joosef and Joel, come to stay."

"You catch more than a spider's web. How do you do it?"

He turned to face her directly. Then she saw his ear. A crust-like patch scabbed his earlobe. It was as if an earring had been ripped out.

"There's a stone missing in your courtyard wall. I sneak through it," he said. "And after you go to bed, I come inside. I help myself to olives and raisins. Bread too, if there is any left over."

"That's stealing," she said.

He put his head down as if waiting to be hit. Sapphira wondered how she could explain about stealing without making him afraid. After a few minutes he lifted his head.

She sat on a stone across from him. "Who are you?"

"Zuka," he answered. "Is taking bread against the law of your God?"

I Wonder . . .

I wonder how you would answer Zuka's question . . .

Praise him, because his name is holy. Let the hearts of those who trust in the LORD be glad.

Psalm 105:3

For Each Other

Look to the
LORD and to his
strength. Always
look to him.

Psalm 105:4

"Tell me your story," Sapphira said. "Then I'll tell you about God's law."

Zuka was quiet for a minute. Then he began. "One day I was put into a cart and covered with heavy mats. I never knew why I was taken from my family except that my father owed money to many people."

"Every day I had to work from sunup until sundown. Then one day a very old man told me that a slave in a Hebrew household always had a day of rest."

"That's what God commands," Sapphira said.

Zuka nodded. "I tried to tell my master that I could work harder and stronger if he gave me a day of rest. But it made him angry. He gave me extra work. So I decided to run away to find out about the God of the Hebrews. The God of good laws."

Sapphira whistled. "Goodness and mercy. What have you learned?"

"Everything I saw and ate spoke to me, telling me that God must be true. I saw a big cat with eyes that glowed. I saw a wild goat nursing her kid. And I ate honey from a rock."

"You've seen more than I have," Sapphira said. "I wish I could travel like that."

"No you don't," Zuka said. "It's lonely. What you have is best."

Sapphira wondered if a heart could be stubbed like a toe. She whispered, "In the beginning, God created two people so that no one would be alone."

I Wonder . . .
I wonder what special people God has put in your life . . .

Creation: Taking Care of God's World
Genesis 2

If you have chores, it means you are special. It means you have been given things that need care. God gave people the whole world to take care of. God trusted us enough to put us in charge. Praise God this week with words from Psalm 8. And thank God for everything that is yours to take care of.

Litany	
Lambs	**Kids**
You made people special.	
	You gave them crowns of glory.
You gave them crowns of honor.	
	You made them rulers—
rulers over all that your hands made,	
	rulers over the animals,
rulers over the birds,	
	and over the fish.
LORD, our LORD,	
	how majestic is your name in the whole earth!

Song for the Week
"This Is My Father's World," *Songs for LiFE* 95

Prayer for the Week
Lord, thank you for the earth you made for us.
Thank you for the people that we share it with.
Help us to know how to live and take care of it all. Amen.

Taking a Chance

LORD, don't hold back your mercy from me.

Psalm 40:11

Sapphira left Zuka with a promise—a promise there'd be food for him on the low, crooked section of the courtyard wall. In her heart, another promise pounded away. She wanted to ask her family about bringing Zuka into their household. But first she'd have to convince her brother, Taavi. And that wouldn't be easy. Taavi wouldn't want a Caananite like Zuka in their home. He'd say the Caananites were cruel, evil people. But Sapphira knew that Zuka was different.

Taavi was pressing olives with the millstone just outside of the courtyard. His face and chest glistened in the sunlight.

"I have our goatskin." She waved it above her head.

"It took you long enough," he said.

She took a deep breath so she'd be careful with her words. The freshly pressed oil filled her nostrils. "You're working hard, Taavi. Have you thought about a helper?"

"There are never enough hands around here. You're running around the hills searching for things you shouldn't have lost. Yerick has the animals to watch. Kyla is useless, and who knows what Jensine and Chana are doing?"

"I'm sorry," Sapphira said. "But I have an answer. A boy named Zuka."

"Zuka?" Taavi filled a basket with olive pulp. "Who's that?" He shoved a clay jar under the basket to collect the oil that seeped out.

Sapphira took a deep breath. "A runaway slave."

I Wonder . . .
I wonder who knew best what Zuka was really like . . .

A Prayer

Sapphira watched Taavi wipe the sweat from his forehead. It seemed forever before he spoke.

"Whose slave was he?"

"I think—I mean, I guess his owner was a Caananite." Sapphira felt a trickle of sweat run down her skin underneath her tunic.

Using a small bowl, Taavi scooped the top layer of oil from a jar. "See this oil," he said. "It's the purest oil. I'm taking it to Eli at the tabernacle tomorrow."

"You didn't answer me about Zuka," she said.

"The oil gives you and me the answer," he said. "It's pure. And you should be too. Don't go mixing yourself up with Caananites."

Sapphira tightened her fingers into a fist. Just because Taavi was the oldest grandson, he thought he was the boss of everything. Well maybe he'd get Grandfather's blessing and the biggest part of all that Grandfather owned, but she wasn't going to listen to him. Not this time. She turned, planning to run back to Zuka.

"Come back," Taavi called. "The sun is setting. It's time to shout across the hills."

Sapphira stopped. The Feast of Trumpets began at sundown. For weeks she'd been waiting to shout thank-yous to God. She didn't want to miss it now. Up on the hills she'd whisper a prayer to God too, asking him to watch over Zuka.

I Wonder . . .

I wonder if there are times when praying is the best thing you can do for someone . . .

LORD . . . May your love and truth always keep me safe.

Psalm 40:11

Shouts

The hills of Ephraim glowed red and golden yellow. Even the dried grasses seemed dressed in glory. All of Grandfather Barzilla and Grandmother Peninah's sons, daughters, and grandchildren marched though the valley between the hills. They stopped between two hills that stood across from each other.

"Come shout to the Lord with me," Cousin Jensine said to Sapphira.

Taavi grabbed Sapphira by the elbow. "No, she's staying with me."

Sapphira wanted to twist away from Taavi's grip. But it was no use. There was no escaping Taavi when his mind was set.

Following her parents, she climbed the hills. Taavi followed right behind her.

At the top of the opposite hill, Uncle Itmar shouted, "Thanks be to God for the land. For the grapes. And for the olives."

Sapphira's father shouted back. "May we always care for the land. For the grapevines. And for the olive trees."

Yerick was next. "Thanks be to God for the lambs and kids. For the sheep and goats."

Sapphira stood to take a turn before Taavi could shout back to Yerick. "Take care of those who are alone. Save those who need you," she said.

Grandfather said her shout was a good one.

I Wonder . . .
I wonder what you would shout to God if you could shout from the hilltops . . .

You are the One [Lord] who helps me and saves me. My God, please don't wait any longer.

Psalm 40:17b

Gone

Sapphira leaped ahead of Taavi on the way home.

A couple of times she flinched, thinking a shadow moved in the distance. Perhaps it was Zuka. But the only creature they met was an owl.

Before getting out her sleeping mat that night, she set out a pitcher of milk for Zuka.

Maybe he was somewhere nearby.

In the morning, the milk pitcher was still full. The smell of sweet-baked bread filled the air—soft loaves made with new olive oil. But Sapphira's family would not eat any of it until after they brought their offerings to the tabernacle.

"Long ago," said her father, "the Lord spoke to Moses. 'On the first day of the seventh month you must have a special service that is announced with trumpet blasts.'"*

"The Feast of Trumpets," Taavi shouted. Then he whispered to Sapphira, "Your Zuka would be like a trapped wild donkey if we took him to the tabernacle."

Taavi was right. Zuka wouldn't know to stand up when Eli read from the law of God. He'd be a half-naked creature without an offering or New Year's clothes.

On the journey to Shiloh, Sapphira watched for Zuka. But again there was no sign of him. Had his master caught him?

Once they were inside the tabernacle, she stood with the grown-ups and joined them in speaking: "This is a great and holy day."

I Wonder . . .
I wonder if you know who was taking care of Zuka . . .

*See Leviticus 23:23

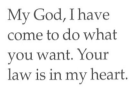

My God, I have come to do what you want. Your law is in my heart.

Psalm 40:8

The Word of God

The next part of the tabernacle celebration filled Sapphira with great fear. Not the kind of fear caused by crossing paths with a bear, but more like the strange feeling you get when you're standing at the top of a high place. It made her stomach tumble. Eli brought out the ark of the covenant with its beautiful golden cherubim. Suddenly the high priest's words caught her attention. "Leave food for poor people and outsiders. I am the Lord your God."

Sapphira looked over to where the men and boys stood. Did Taavi hear that?

Quivering blasts sounded from the ram's horn trumpets. First long, then short.

Now it was time to feast and taste the sweet honey of the new year.

On the way out of the tabernacle Taavi yanked on Sapphira's arm. "Come with me," he said. "I think your little friend is lurking in the bushes. Tell him he doesn't belong."

Shaking, she followed Taavi. But before they went more than a stone's throw, a man reached out and grabbed Taavi by the throat.

"Return our slave, boy," said the man, who cast a large dark shadow.

Sapphira stepped forward. "We're looking for him too."

"Stole from you, did he?" The man hissed as he slowly let go of Taavi.

Sadness filled Sapphira's heart. Zuka couldn't stay with them after all. It wouldn't be safe for him. But she would do what she could. She could leave him food. And always be on the lookout.

I Wonder . . .
I wonder how God can use you to help others . . .

Many people will see what he [the Lord] has done and will worship him. They will put their trust in the LORD.

Psalm 40:3b

Sin Spoils God's World
Genesis 3

Imagine you are giving a party. You buy the food, the drinks, and the decorations. You spend hours selecting the best games and prizes. But when your guests arrive, they don't even look at your games and decorations. They go into your parents' room—the one place in the house that's off-limits. Your party is ruined.

God created a perfect world. But one day the people God had made walked right past all the good things and went to the tree that God told them to stay away from. They disobeyed. Now God's perfect world was ruined. It's a wonder God didn't walk away from the people.

But it's even a bigger wonder that God planned and prepared a gift that was even greater than the gift of the world.

Echo the words from Romans 5: 15, 17, 21.

Litany	
Lambs	**Kids**
One man sinned.	
	Death ruled because of his sin.
But God's grace came through another man.	
	That man is Jesus Christ.
Jesus, the grace of God, brings eternal life.	
	We have life because of what Jesus Christ has done.

Song for the Week
"Come, Thou Long-Expected Jesus," *Songs for LiFE* 122

Prayer for the Week
Lord, thank you for the gift of your Son.
Thank you for forgiving our sins
because of your Son. The gift of your Son is so
great that we can never stop saying thank you. Amen.

Secrets in a Hole

Jensine climbed the steps to the rooftop of their house. The evening stars came up like sparks from a fire. She counted the stars like Yerick counted his sheep.

Dots of light from oil lamps flickered on rooftops across Bethel. The soft bleating of the sheep and goats drifted up from the courtyard. Yerick was bedding them down for the night.

Just then a shadowy figure moved alongside the wall directly below. It was Jensine's oldest sister, Kyla. She held something against the folds of her robe.

Kyla stopped and shifted a rock. Jensine noticed a hole in the ground where the rock had been. Kyla paused, then lifted a carved stone object. A Caananite idol god! Jensine pressed herself against the small wall around the rooftop edges.

Kyla set the idol on the ground. With tapping steps she danced in a small circle around the idol. Then facing the rising moon, she stretched her arms upward. Her long black hair shimmered under the silver light, and her face shone as white as milk. Jensine often wished for beauty like Kyla's, but now it scared her.

Where had Kyla learned how to worship idols? An image of Kyla speaking in hushed words to their mother sent shivers over Jensine's skin. Had Mother brought the Caananite worship to their Israelite home?

I Wonder . . .
I wonder what you would do if you were Jensine . . .

People of Israel,
the LORD's arm
is not too weak to
save you.

Isaiah 59:1

Overheard

Jensine curled up into a ball. She couldn't look anymore. What was in Kyla's heart? Keeping her knees tucked against her body helped the shaking a bit. But the moonlit dancing image haunted her.

Footsteps slapped against the rooftop stairs. Quickly Jensine crouched behind a tall storage jar.

Voices came within hearing distance.

"Did you hide the idol?" It was Mother speaking to Kyla.

So it was an idol for sure. Mother missed the Feast of the Trumpets celebration because of a visit to her Caananite relatives. Did she bring the idol back with her? Her mother spent more and more time in the Caananite city of Megiddo. Father wore a worried look each time she left. And Grandmother Peninah walked around with lips pressed together.

Jensine wished that squeezing out the troubling thoughts would make them go away. Mother devoted so much attention to Kyla. Didn't Mother love all of her girls? And wouldn't she do what was best for them?

"You must please this god," Mother said to Kyla. "Then you will be more beautiful than ever."

"Did you bring me the paint for my eyes?" Kyla asked.

"It's in this alabaster jar—just one of the lovely things you'll see in Megiddo."

I Wonder ...
I wonder if there's someone in your life that you're worried about . . .

But your sins have separated you from your God.

Isaiah 59:2

The Plan

Jensine stayed behind the storage jars. The swish of Mother's robe stirred the air. And the scent of her small myrrh bag filled Jensine's nose.

Kyla moved toward Jensine's hiding place. "I'll hide the eye paint in a granary jar."

Jensine didn't move a finger or a toe even though her legs tingled.

"Are we going to tell Father?" Kyla asked.

"Touch my face, my child. Do you feel how beautiful I am? You are like me. Your nose is elegant. Your eyes are dark like wine. We deserve better things than we can find here."

"But Father married you because you were beautiful."

Jensine's mother laughed—a laugh that rang out like a bronze cup falling on a stone. "Your father was handsome too. That's why I fell in love with him. But living in Bethel isn't as exciting as Megiddo. Worshiping only one god isn't enough for me."

She laughed again. The laugh rattled in Jensine's ears.

"Old Barzilla and his stories about Abraham, Isaac, and Jacob are growing tiresome," said her mother.

Jensine thought about what made her the happiest. It was Grandfather's stories, the trips to Shiloh, and the warm touch of Grandmother's bread-making hands.

I Wonder . . .
I wonder when keeping secrets in a family is a good thing . . .
A bad thing . . .

Those people weave their evil plans together like a spider's web. . . . Their acts are evil.

Isaiah 59:6

Pain

Jensine stayed crouched behind the jar long after Mother and Kyla left. She wasn't sure what her mother had planned. Was Mother returning to the Caananite way of life—turning her back on God?

If Jensine jumped up now and ran into her mother's arms, what would happen? She loved Mother. But did Mother love her plain-looking Jensine? Tears slipped down her face.

Clouds covered the moon of the seventh month. Her heart felt as if a millstone pressed down on her chest.

What would Grandfather do? Grandfather's stories ran through her mind. In all those stories it was God who came to the rescue. Jensine looked up into the heavens. The clouds scurried as if they were being chased. The moonlight shone so brightly that the entire rooftop seemed full of light.

The light! That was the answer and the story that she needed. Tomorrow she'd tell Kyla.

Jensine layed down. She slept until soft sheep bleats woke her. Immediately she sat up. By the way her head felt, it could have been stuffed with sheep's wool. And why was she sleeping up on the rooftop without a mat? Then she remembered. And the sadness of last night became real again.

I Wonder . . .
I wonder if you know how it feels when there's sadness in your family . . .

They are always in a hurry to sin. . . . They leave a trail of suffering and pain.

Isaiah 59:7

The One True God

In the morning, Jensine found Kyla rubbing oil into her skin, making it soft.

"May I sit by you?" Jensine asked.

"Please yourself," Kyla answered.

"Last night the moon was as bright as the sun," Jensine said, sitting close to her sister. "It made me think of God leading Moses and the people out of Egypt."

Kyla poured more oil into her cupped hand.

Jensine took a deep breath and continued. "Only the true God would save his people like that. Just imagine—God led our people with a pillar of light." Jensine prayed in her heart before continuing. "Caananites have slaves carrying their lights. But God carried our light. What a difference! Right?"

Oil dribbled through Kyla's fingers. For a minute, a troubled wrinkle crossed her forehead. "What are you trying to tell me?"

Jensine picked up the bowl of oil. She held it out towards Kyla. "Our God is so good. When we need help, the Lord takes care of us better than a slave could."

As quick as a cloud that covers the sun, Kyla's face changed. It looked like stone. "You know so little," she said. "Someday I'll be a queen with slaves who do everything for me. Let's see God do that." Then she picked up the oil bowl and left.

Jensine knew it was goodbye.

I Wonder . . .
I wonder if there's anyone you know who can care for you better than God can . . .

They lead twisted lives. No one who lives like that will enjoy peace and rest.

Isaiah 59:8b

Cain and Abel

Genesis 4:1-16

How can we show God we're sorry for our sins? We can tell God we're sorry when we pray each day. We can show God we're sorry by the things we do and say.

In Cain and Abel's time, God's people had to do more than say they were sorry. They had to bring God something of value—something called a sacrifice.

Why don't we need to give sacrifices to God today? Because when Jesus died on the cross, he became our sacrifice—the most perfect sacrifice of all. And he did it for you and me and everyone who loves him.

Give thanks this week that Jesus' sacrifice was big enough for all of his people. These words from Revelation 5:12 will help you do that.

Litany	
Lambs	**Kids**
The Lamb is worthy!	
	He is worthy
to receive power	
	and wisdom
and strength!	
	He is worthy
to receive honor	
	and glory and praise.

Song for the Week
"Worthy Is Christ," *Songs for LiFE* 170

Prayer for the Week
Thank you, Lord Jesus, for being our perfect Lamb.
Your life for mine. Thank you with all the praise I can give. Amen.

A Goat for Sins?

Yerick thought about his goats. There was Ofer, the gentle one; Phizibah, the potbellied one; and the twins, Gillie and Giza, who liked to play rough. And then there was Muppem, the one who leaped when Yerick was happy and who nuzzled when he was sad.

Father said Eli had asked their family to supply the goats this year. Yerick pulled his shepherd's hood down over his eyes. He didn't want to think of losing any of his goats. If only he could find some old ornery goats to bring to the tabernacle tomorrow.

He whistled a long note and two short ones through the space between his front teeth. Usually his sheep and goats lined up for the fields when he gave this special call. What was wrong this morning? They huddled around the manger of dried grass. Didn't they want to go out for fresh grass?

"Shoo! Shoo!" he called, trying to scatter them away from the manger.

Suddenly, his cousin Jensine popped up in the middle of the manger. Pieces of dried grass stuck out from her hair and clothes. Her eyes were red too. What was wrong with Jensine?

"Yerick," she said in her soft voice, "will one of your goats really take away all of our sins?"

I Wonder . . .
I wonder if you know who takes your sins away . . .

He suffered the things we should have suffered.

Isaiah 53:4

Without Sin?

Yerick stroked Ofer's smooth white coat.

"Is Ofer the goat to take away sins?" Jensine asked.

Yerick stepped in front of Ofer. "Any goat should be fine. I don't know why it has to be one of mine. I put a lot of work into my goats—bringing them to the best pastures, brushing their coats, and protecting them from harm."

"That's why Eli needs one of yours," Jensine said. "He needs a perfect one."

"Perhaps I can trade a donkey for a goat that would be just right. Someone in Gilgal or Ramah might have one."

Jensine studied the loose threads of a hole in her tunic. "You wouldn't know anything about someone else's goat. It might be stubborn or have a disease."

"So?"

"God says it must be a perfect goat to take our sins away."

Jensine's soft clay-brown eyes were gentle, innocent, even though there was a troubling look of panic in them. Surely Jensine never did anything wrong. And Yerick couldn't think of a single sin he had done either. Why did they have to worry so much about a sacrifice?

"I can't think of a th-single th-sin for you or me." He hated it when his whistle came between his teeth when he didn't want it to. But that wasn't a sin.

I Wonder . . .

I wonder if there's anyone in your family who has *never* done anything wrong . . .

> He took on himself the pain that should have been ours.
>
> *Isaiah 53:4b*

Jensine's Sadness

Yerick whistled three short notes as a signal for the goats and sheep to spread out in the field. They sniffed around for juicy clumps of grass.

Jensine untied a four-cornered knot in her cloth. She spread out thick slices of cheese, sweet figs, and fat shriveled olives. "This is for you," she said.

Yerick sat beside her on the hillside. "You're always giving to others. God can't have anything against you."

Jensine swiped her hand across the bottom of her nose. "Yerick, yesterday while you were in the fields, a chariot came. It was pulled by two strong horses."

"Where was it from?" he asked.

"Megiddo! The driver came to pick up Kyla and Mother. Kyla laughed at me when I begged her to stay. She said in Megiddo she could worship Baal *and* our God."

"Are they coming back?" Yerick asked.

The colored sides of the chariot, the jewels on the horses, and the way the driver kissed her mother and sister flashed through her mind. "I think Kyla will worship Baal so she can have jewels and colored robes. That will make the Lord God angry with her. I have to know if her sin can be taken away. I must know if she can come back to us."

I Wonder . . .

I wonder if Mother and Kyla *really* can worship both Baal and our God . . .

But the servant was pierced because we had sinned. He was crushed because we had done what was evil.

Isaiah 53:5

Secrets of the Heart

Yerick wished he could take the sadness out of Jensine's round eyes. But the sadness was greater than one of his cheery words—it was a pain that he couldn't remove. What would he do if his mother had chosen all those fine things over being his mother?

Jensine reached for one of Muppem's ears. "When I touched the smooth sides of the chariot, I shook. Mother and Kyla will never return to Bethel. All Bethel has are crooked little houses."

There was a hush between them. A long, heavy silence that matched the haze from the seventh month's heat.

It was Aunt Masika and cousin Kyla's sin against God that hurt Jensine.

"There's more," Jensine said. "It's what was in my heart. As the horse pranced away and the chariot wheels spun around, I wanted to be with them. I was ready to sit beside mother and have her promise me beautiful robes and jewels. In the secret place of my heart, I wanted it more than I wanted God."

The words about secret places in the heart jabbed Yerick. Ten days ago when Taavi brought the oil to the Tabernacle, Eli had blessed Taavi. Yerick wished he had thrown sand into Taavi's oil.

Muppem rubbed her chin against Yerick's leg. Yerick trembled. He knew there was sin in him too. Secret sin trying to hide its face, taking him away from God.

He was punished to make us whole again. His wounds have healed us.

Isaiah 53:5b

I Wonder . . .

I wonder if you know what Jensine means when she talks about a "secret place in her heart" . . .

I wonder if you have secret places in your heart too . . .

Two Goats

Yerick fought to breathe as Eli tossed the yes and no stones for the goats. The first yes stone chose Ofer. Before he followed Eli to the altar, Ofer looked at Yerick with gentle eyes. Eli lifted his knife to let out the life blood in Ofer.

A dizzy circle spun in Yerick's head. Of all that God had given the world, of all that God had created, life was the most precious. Life with the laughter and love that it gave. Yet there wasn't life without forgiveness from God. Yerick knew he needed it. But right now the painful price of sin seemed greater than the peace of forgiveness.

The next yes stone landed on Muppem. Now she was the scape goat, the goat that had to carry away their sins. Yerick could imagine Muppem alone, wandering through the desert. He whispered in Muppem's ear. "If you see a sea of deep blue water in the desert, don't drink it. The salt in the sea will bite you like a rat."

Then he held Muppem in his arms. And he cried. Muppem licked his tears as if to say, "I'll do it. I'll do it for you, for Jensine, and all the people."

Eli placed his hands on Muppem. "Carry away our sins. Just as we'll never see you again, may we never see our sins again."

Yerick looked away. As he did, he saw Jensine. Tears streaked down her face. And he wished for peace for Jensine, Chana, and Martha, his motherless cousins.

I Wonder . . .
I wonder when you feel the sadness of sin in your life . . .

All of us have turned to our own way. And the LORD has placed on his servant the sins of all of us.

Isaiah 53:6b

Rain and Rainbows

Genesis 6:5-9:17

"Never again." That's what God told Noah. "Never again will I destroy all living things." To help Noah and his children remember this promise, God made a picture in the sky. God told Noah that whenever there was a rainbow in the sky, it would shout God's promise all over again. I wonder how many rainbows have appeared since the time of Noah?

This week repeat God's promise from Genesis 8:22. Think about rainbows each time you say it.

Litany	
Lambs	**Kids**
As long as the earth lasts,	
	there will always be a time to plant.
As long as the earth lasts,	
	there will be a time to gather the crops.
As long as the earth lasts,	
	there will be cold and heat.
As long as the earth lasts,	
	there will be summer and winter.
As long as the earth lasts,	
	There will be day and night.

Song for the Week
"Come, Let Us Gather," *Songs for LiFE* 2

Prayer for the Week
God of promises,
God of rainbows,
you are my God.
Thank you for saving me. Amen.

The Feast of Booths

Everywhere Yerick looked tree-branch tents were scattered across the hills. The temple of Shiloh rose above them all on the highest hill—Mount Ephraim. Celebrating the Festival of Booths was a happy time. Or at least it should be. Father had taught Yerick the words Moses said long ago: "You must be filled with joy in my sight for seven days. I am the LORD your God" (Lev. 23:40b).

Living in a tent for seven days made Yerick thankful for his home in Bethel, but there was an ache in his heart. It was only five days ago since the Day of Atonement—the day when sins were paid for—the day when he gave up Ofer and Muppem.

Yerick watched as Jensine twirled leafy branches near a booth tent. She seemed to have peace about God's forgiveness. And even a bit of hope that her mother and Kyla might come back someday. "Whistle your dancing tune," she said.

Last year he was called the sweet piper as his cousins skipped and danced to his music. But this year everything felt different. "It's not in me," he said.

Jensine's eyes rounded in a quiet sadness. And before Yerick could explain his mixed-up feelings, a group of girls swept Jensine away. She joined the parade of people following Eli.

Yerick tagged behind the edges of the large group. He watched as Eli poured water from the golden pitcher over the altar. The people raised shouts of joy. Evening torches were lit and dancing began. Unable to find Jensine, Yerick went back to his booth.

I Wonder . . .
I wonder what it will take for Yerick to be happy again . . .

God, show us
your favor. Bless
us. May you
smile on us
with your favor.

Psalm 67:1

Wild Goats?

In the morning, drops of rain fell through the booth branches. Yesterday's prayers for rain were being answered already. It was a good sign. Perhaps God would send the right amount of rain this season.

No one seemed to mind eating breakfast in the drizzle. After all, they came to pray for rain this week as well as to thank God for the harvest of last year.

Yerick picked up an olive branch left over from the booth building. It was the right height and was curved perfectly to make a shepherd's staff. He removed the bottom branches with his flint knife, leaving the top leaves in place. Now he had a festive-looking staff. Maybe he could find some joy this week, after all.

"I didn't see you at the torch dances last night," he said to Jensine.

She looked up in surprise. "I didn't think you went."

Before he could explain, she jumped up. "What's that over there?" She pointed to a jagged group of rocks.

He studied the mound of rocks. Something moved. Yerick leaped in that direction. Two young goats nibbled on a bush. They were the funniest pair of goats he had ever seen. A male and a female. One was black with a brown patch over its left eye, and the other was brown with a black patch over its right eye.

I Wonder . . .

I wonder how many ways you can name in which God has answered your prayers this week . . .

May all the people on earth praise you.

Psalm 67:3b

Black and Brown, Brown and Black

Yerick stretched out his hand to the goats.

"I wonder who they belong to?" Jensine asked.

He scanned the hills. "I don't see anyone around. I'm sure no one in Bethel owns goats with this coloring. I'd remember these two."

"Do you suppose they are wild goats?" Jensine asked.

Yerick scratched the black one under its chin. "This one is tame," he said. "I'd better look for the owner." Then he patted the brown one. It bumped against his thigh.

"They act as if they like you," Jensine said. "Why don't you give them names?"

Naming goats was fun. But if he did, it would feel as if they belonged to him. "No, I have to find the owner. Come along with me."

"I can't," Jensine said. "I mean—there's something else I want to do. Besides, it's raining." She ran off, leaving him with the two goats.

Yerick gave a short whistle, and the goats skipped along beside him.

The Gilgal camp was the closest to the Bethel camp, so he decided to begin there. The people in the Gilgal camp still had dancing left in their feet. The silvery sheet of rain only seemed to make them happier. Yerick explained the goats to the first man he met.

"Those are goats I'd remember," the man said. "However, your story about finding goats reminds me of times when God blesses us with unexpected love."

I Wonder . . .

I wonder if you can think of a time when God surprised you with an unexpected blessing . . .

You rule the
people of the
earth fairly.

Psalm 67:4b

Anatie and Zimra

Next Yerick met a boy guiding his flock out to a patch of grass. "Nice goats," said the boy. "Where did they come from?"

"I found them in the rocks," Yerick said.

"You must have saved them," the boy said. "That means they belong to you."

More than anything Yerick wanted to believe that.

Before he went much farther, the rain stopped. As if by command, the sun came out, and a rainbow arched across the sky.

"Lovely, isn't it?"

He turned to see an old woman carrying olive branches.

She set her bundle of wood on the ground. "You remind me of Noah, with that pair of goats and the branch from the olive tree."

Yerick thought about the pairs of animals coming to Noah. And how the first branch brought to Noah was from the olive tree. God was in control then. Did God know about this rainbow and these goats too?

He decided it would be fun to give them names for now. Anatie for the brown one. It meant "singer." And Zimra, "a song," for the black one. The names fit with the song starting in his heart.

But first he needed to go to Ramah. He hoped the answers about the goats would be the same there.

I Wonder . . .

I wonder how it makes you feel to know that God is in control of everything that happens in your life . . .

God, our God,
will bless us.

Psalm 67:6b

A Full Song

God will bless us.
People from one
end of the earth to
the other will have
respect for him.

Psalm 67:7

The Ramah camp was quiet. A few bleating goats guided Yerick to a makeshift pen. Almost like a thief he crept up to the animals. There they were—black and brown goats. And not just solid colors, but blacks and browns mixed together—copies of Anatie and Zimra.

Not far away under a nearby booth, a baby cried. The soothing voice of a young girl sang a lullaby. Why did that voice seem so familiar?

The branches hung low over the booth so he couldn't see inside. He lifted the corner of a branch. And there was Jensine. A baby was riding on her hip, and two young children were clinging to her tunic.

Why was she caring for these children while their parents were celebrating? Maybe the parents were paying her something valuable.

The goats! Of course! Anatie and Zimra didn't just end up in the rocks by themselves. Suddenly it made sense that Jensine had put them there.

Yerick whistled her favorite tune. The baby stopped crying.

"Meet a singer and a song—Anatie and Zimra," he said. "It seems as if I've been given more than I gave God. All because you put these goats in the rocks for me."

"It's because of God," Jensine said. "When I knew God made me new because of forgiveness, I saw God's blessings everywhere. It made me want to share."

I Wonder . . .
I wonder if you can think of a time that you felt so thankful that you wanted to share . . .

The Tallest Tower

Genesis 11:1-9

The world is very big and very great. And God gives us many choices in this wide creation. There are many things we can do and places we can go. But whatever we decide to do, we need to depend on God. We need to put God first.

So don't be like the people who built the tower of Babel. They thought they could get power on their own. They forgot that they needed God.

Litany	
Lambs	**Kids**
Trust in the LORD	
	with all your heart.
Trust in the LORD.	
	Do not depend on your own understanding.
In all your ways remember him.	
	Then he will make your paths smooth and straight.

Song for the Week
"Trust in the Lord," *Songs for LiFE* 212

Prayer for the Week
Lord, teach us how to depend on you.
Take us on your paths. Amen.

Plans

Kyla curled up on a dirty mat in a small house in Megiddo. Her mother had left her there two days ago. She wasn't quite sure what was happening. Her mother said it was just for now, just until some important matters were settled.

Kyla covered her ears. That shut out most of the nighttime noise of the city. But it didn't erase the screams that she heard inside of her head.

She flipped over to the other side of her grimy mat. Other children slept close beside her. Flies landed on their sleeping bodies but didn't wake them. The rotting smell of garbage filled the room.

As soon as it quieted down for the night, Kyla planned to escape. She would find her way back to Bethel—no matter how long it took. Did Jensine miss her? Was Grandfather Barzilla worried about her? If only she could hear Grandmother Peninah say, "Bless this child."

Kyla felt herself breathing too fast. Keep calm, she repeated over and over. Finally the night sounds faded. She stood up on her mat. Carefully she stepped over the sleeping children and out of the small house. It was quiet in the streets. Almost as quiet as it was two nights ago when she overheard her mother talking to a man decorated with pieces of bone and ivory. Thinking back on that conversation, she guessed that her mother planned to sell her.

I Wonder . . .
I wonder which words from God stay with you when you are in trouble . . .

Don't let love and truth ever leave you. Tie them around your neck. Write them on the tablet of your heart.

Proverbs 3:3

Not Enough

In Megiddo, merchants sold cinnamon and balm. And daily, traders came with fine things. Kyla's mother's family greedily bought more and more beautiful things for themselves. At first it seemed wonderful. But then they ran into a big problem. The grain they had set aside for planting new crops had been used or stolen, and there was no money to replace it. So Kyla's mother's relatives were angry. They yelled at each other. Soon there was no one who didn't blame another person.

No matter how poor times seemed in Bethel, it had never turned out like this. Even if there was a small bit of flour for supper, Kyla's family gave thanks for it. Giving thanks always brought happiness even when the loaf of bread was small. They depended on God. And somehow if there wasn't wheat, there was barley. Or there was milk from the goats.

Never, never would they think of selling anyone as a slave to make up the difference. If someone did get into deep trouble—trouble like Kyla's mother's family faced here in Megiddo—Eli was always there to judge fairly.

Kyla moved toward the horse stables, using the walls as a guide. She'd hide out in the stables. In the darkest part of the night, she'd make her way down the steep hill of Megiddo. Then she'd find her way to Shechem or Shiloh and back to Bethel.

Why did she ever think that beauty was all that she needed? For the first time Kyla began to understand Jensine's happiness. It came from deep inside.

I Wonder . . .
I wonder if you know what it means to feel happiness from deep inside . . .

Honor the LORD with your wealth. Give him the first share of all your crops. Then your storerooms will be so full they can't hold everything.

Proverbs 3:9-10a

A Hiding Place

The LORD is the one you will trust in. He will keep your feet from being caught in a trap.

Proverbs 3:26

Kyla stopped in her path. A noise followed her. Footsteps crunched against the loose stones in the street. No doubt about it, she was being followed. The sides of her neck throbbed.

With the swiftness she had learned from playing with her cousins, she fled for the stables. She went straight to Nur's stall. This black horse had become her friend. He learned to trust her after she nursed his wounds from a chariot driver's whip.

"Protect me, Nur," she whispered. Then she crawled under the hay in Nur's feeding trough. She flattened herself deep inside the carved-out stone.

"I'm positive she came into the stables," said a voice.

"She's gone now," answered an irritated voice. "But even if she gets out of the city, there's nowhere for her to go. From what her mother says, her family would never take her back. A regular little princess who acts as if she's better than others."

"Yeah," said the first voice. "But she's the kind that'll serve well in Baal's temple. The kind that'll do what you want with the promise of a trinket or two."

The men left. She was safe. But what did it matter now? The men were right. She had turned her back on her sisters and cousins and her God just because she wanted a few beautiful things. If only she knew then what she knew now. If only the one true God could be her one and only God again.

I Wonder . . .
I wonder if it's too late for God to be Kyla's one and only God again . . .

A Prayer

Kyla tried to remember the prayers of Grandfather and Jensine. Their words made great and beautiful prayers. But where should she begin? Sometimes Grandfather fell down on his face, saying he couldn't speak God's name because God was so holy. Yet God wasn't like Baal. Kyla knew she didn't have to slice herself with a knife to make God listen. Neither did she have to dance in wild circles or sell herself to the priests.

God protected the people. Wasn't that what Jensine tried to tell her on that last day in Bethel? The Lord God loved them. And God would keep them from harm. Unlike the demands of the Baal priests, the true God's laws were for their safety.

"Forgive me," she whispered. "If I had listened to Jensine telling me that you were the only God, I wouldn't be in this trouble." Then she took a deep breath. "Go with me," she said, feeling as if her whole life was in God's hands.

Nur nudged her. She rolled out of the feeding trough. "Nur, I'm going home. It's the only thing left for me to do."

Nur pawed his foot against the ground. Kyla reached up and stroked his face.

"I'm sorry I can't take you with me. Taavi and Yerick would love to have you. But neither of us would make it out alive if we left together."

Nur nuzzled her arm as if he understood. Then she slipped past the other horses, climbed the outside stable wall, and dropped to the ground just outside of Megiddo.

I Wonder . . .
I wonder when it's easiest to trust ourselves . . .
I wonder when it's easiest to trust God . . .

Trust in the LORD with all your heart. Do not depend on your own understanding.

Proverbs 3:5

The Path Home

In all your ways remember him. Then he will make your paths smooth and straight.

Proverbs 3:6

Kyla hurried down the steep hillside. In her haste, she forgot to zigzag down the straight slope. She skidded until a small tree stopped her. A fast-growing lump rose up on her forehead. But she knew it wouldn't help to feel sorry for herself. The rest of the night, she worked her way down the hill in a sitting position.

In the morning, the sun guided her southward. But soon hunger and dizziness took over, and before long Kyla fell to the ground.

"Great thunder and lightening!" called out a voice. "What do we have here?" The man stopped beside Kyla and lifted up her head, giving her a drink of water. "It looks as if you belong back in Megiddo. Here, I'll bring you back on my horse."

Suddenly Kyla caught on to what the man was saying. "No," she shouted, jumping up. She didn't know how long she ran or in which direction.

Another man who was riding a donkey stopped her. She tried to run again, but this time she had no more strength. The man picked her up and cradled her in his arms. "Kyla, my precious baby," he whispered.

The familiar voice and smell of the man gave her a shekel of strength. "Father?"

"Hush." He brushed his hand gently over her lips. "The Lord has tested you. Do you love God with all your heart and with all your soul?"

"I do, Father," she whispered.

I Wonder...
I wonder what Kyla's father meant when he said, "The Lord has tested you"...

Abraham and Sarah Believe God's Promises

Genesis 11:31-12:9

God promised Abraham a son. To find out if God gave Abraham the promised son, you just have to read a few chapters in the book of Genesis. But Abraham didn't have it so easy. He had to wait twenty-five years. How old would you be if you had to wait for a promise for twenty-five years from today?

Some promises from God seem to take a long time. Can you trust God while you wait? It helps when you read the stories of Abraham and other believers.

Use the words from Psalm 77:11-12 to remind yourself to remember that God keeps promises.

Litany	
Lambs	**Kids**
LORD, I will remember what you did.	
	Yes, I will remember your miracles of long ago.
I will spend time thinking about everything you have done.	
	I will consider all of your mighty acts.

Song for the Week
"We Are on Our Way," *Songs for LiFE* 100

Prayer for the Week
Lord, your promises make us glad
because your promises are not just words.
Your promises are there for our hope
and for good in our life. Amen.

A Closed and Guarded City

Zuka smelled the baking of the evening bread. His stomach rumbled. He hoped Sapphira would set out two loaves this evening.

As the stars came up, he gave them names—Sapphira, Yerick, Jensine, Chana, Martha, Joosef, and Joel. He stopped the naming before he came to Kyla and Taavi. Thinking about Kyla made him scared for her. But thinking about Taavi made him scared for himself. Would Taavi always say that a Canaanite boy was not welcome in Bethel?

The last star he sighted was for Grandfather Barzilla. This star was his sign that it was late enough to sneak into Bethel for his supper.

After all these weeks of collecting his supper, Zuka had worn a path to the hole in Bethel's wall. So it took him by surprise to find tonight that the wall was patched. Was it done on purpose to keep him out, or had someone just gotten around to fixing it?

He ran to the gate. Even if the gate was closed, it was easy enough to slip inside. But as he neared the gate, Zuka saw Abisha, Jensine's father, guarding the entrance.

Zuka stumbled over to a nearby stone pile. They must have found out that he was a thief and a . . . He couldn't bring himself to say the awful names about himself. For weeks he had wanted the good things Sapphira talked about. He should have known better. God's promises were for people like Sapphira, not for him.

I Wonder . . .
I wonder if God's promises are for Zuka too . . .
I wonder if God's promises are for you . . .

Like a lost sheep, I've gone down the wrong path. Come and look for me.

Psalm 119:176

A Light

Zuka picked at the scab on his arm. The red, crusty patch was still firmly attached. He tugged anyway. The blood oozed out, reminding him of the tumble that caused the wound. A leopard had chased him for miles before forcing him down the mountain.

That fall hurt a lot, but it seemed like nothing compared to the pain that filled him now. Every hungry night and every narrow escape had never seemed like an end. Now it was the end. His hope was gone.

He might as well just lie here. Sooner or later his accusers would find him and do what they wanted with him.

Zuka lifted his head toward Bethel to say his last goodbye. A light from the rooftop winked on and off as if a hand passed up and down in front of a lamp.

Could it be a signal? With each wink, his hope grew stronger. He needed to send back a signal. The rock badger's whistle! Sapphira would recognize it.

Zuka blew enough breath through his dry mouth to send out an e-e-e-e-k.

In answer, the speed of the winking light went faster. Zuka didn't care who heard him. He yelped with joy.

Then he heard the scraping sound of stone against stone. The gate to Bethel was opening. He took it as an invitation. Sapphira stood beside her Uncle Abisha. They motioned him to come into the courtyard. Then Abisha closed the gate. Zuka was inside.

I Wonder . . .
I wonder if you know what it means that God's Word is like a light that guides our way . . .

> Your word is like a lamp that shows me the way. It is like a light that guides me.
>
> *Psalm 119:105*

A Safe Place

Zuka took the bowl of warm water that Sapphira handed him. He put it to his lips.

"No," she said. "That's for washing your hands. I have lentil stew and bread for you to eat."

Zuka put the bowl down. His hand were dirty. Usually his hungry stomach kept him from noticing such things. He put his hands into the warm water. It was worth it when he saw the steaming bowl of food and hunk of bread that Sapphira handed him.

Sapphira gave thanks to God in heaven for the food. Every part of Zuka wanted to give thanks too, right down to his toes.

Between gulps of food, he looked around. Grandfather Barzilla and Sapphira's Uncle Abisha spoke in low voices by the gate. What was wrong?

"Bethel," he whispered to Sapphira. "Is it in danger?"

Sapphira moved a bit closer to him. "My cousin Kyla came home. She escaped—left Megiddo. And my aunt had sold her, so she wasn't free to go. Someone from Megiddo may be looking for her. But now that she's home, she'll be safe. Grandfather and all of us will make sure of that."

The courtyard walls shielded against the outside like a blanket protecting against the cold. And then there was Grandfather and Abisha adding their protection. It felt so good Zuka wanted to cry. He had never cried when he got hurt or when he was scared. But the safe feeling was so big, he couldn't hold it inside.

I Wonder . . .
I wonder what makes you feel safe . . .

You are my place of safety. You are like a shield that keeps me safe. I have put my hope in your word.

Psalm 119:114

The Truth About Zuka

Zuka was glad that it was too dark for Sapphira to see him crying. But she wasn't the kind of person you could fool for very long. So, as much as he wanted to ask her if he could stay, he knew that it would be goodbye after the stew was gone.

"Would you like me to fill up your bowl again?" she asked.

He held it out.

Before she came back, Taavi walked into the courtyard. A knife blade hanging below his belt flashed in the moonlight.

"So it's Zuka," he said with a mocking laugh. "There's a reward out for you. The way I figure, it could be mine as well as anyone else's."

"You wouldn't!" shouted Sapphira, as Taavi ran his fingers over his knife blade.

"Has your little friend told you why he is wanted?"

Zuka looked straight into Sapphira's innocent, clay-brown eyes. She'd probably protect him without thinking of her own safety. "Taavi's right," he said. "I'm trouble. It's not a good idea for you to help me."

"Tell her about the man you killed," Taavi said.

Zuka wished the ground could swallow him. He couldn't stand to be such a disappointment in Sapphira's eyes. Would she give him a chance to explain the whole story?

I Wonder . . .
I wonder what Zuka's story might be . . .

Keep me going as you have promised. Then I will live. Don't let me lose all hope.

Psalm 119:116

More Than Walls

Zuka waited for Sapphira to scream or run.

"I don't believe it," she said. "You don't have that kind of heart."

Zuka caught his breath in surprise. How could Sapphira know his heart? He had learned long ago that people only thought the worst of a person like him. Could it be true that she would believe him?

"There were two of us," he said, "cutting wood for our master. The other boy's ax flew off the handle. It hit our master and killed him. I ran up to our master to see if he was okay. While I was doing that, the other boy traded my ax for his handle. Then he ran and told the owner that I was the one who killed our master."

Sapphira searched his face as if looking for the truth in his eyes. "Grandfather will take you to Shechem," she said.

Zuka gripped the stick he always carried with him. Why would Sapphira send him to Shechem? Was his story too hard to believe after all? His heart and mind no longer had the energy to tell his feet to run. Besides, Grandfather and Abisha guarded the gate. He held out his hands so Taavi could bind them up.

But Taavi just walked away.

"Shechem is a city of refuge," Sapphira said. "Joshua, the one who led our people into this land, set apart certain cities. God's law will protect you better than city walls" (see Deut. 19:2-7).

There it was again. Sapphira making him think God's promises were for him.

I Wonder . . .
I wonder what made Taavi decide to walk away . . .

Don't leave me
to those who
beat me down.

Psalm 119:121

God's Promise Comes True

Genesis 18:1-15; 21:1-7

Do you like it when something is too hard for you? It may be your spelling words, your math, or getting along with a certain person. It is upsetting to feel you can't do something, isn't it? But sometimes those experiences help us understand what God does for us: God makes the impossible, possible!

Sarah thought it was too hard to have a baby when she was old. In fact, she knew it was impossible. But then it happened, and Sarah knew that God is good. She learned that nothing is impossible with God.

The words of Jeremiah 32:17 remind us of our God, who makes the impossible, possible.

Litany	
Lambs	**Kids**
LORD and King,	
	you have made the heavens.
LORD and King,	
	you have made the earth.
Nothing is too hard for you.	
	Nothing is too hard for you.

Song for the Week
"My God Is So Great," *Songs for LiFE* 35

Prayer for the Week
Jesus, when something is hard, I wonder how I can do it.
From your words I know how hard it is to get to heaven.
I can see you are good to me because you offer me the impossible. Amen.

Trust or Chance

Zuka told the ax story to Grandfather.

"If your story is true," Grandfather said, "you will be protected for the rest of your life. You will be able to live peacefully in Shechem."

"Can we take Zuka to Shechem now?" Sapphira asked.

"In the morning," Grandfather said. "Your Uncle Gersham can take him. All the other men must stay in Bethel to protect Kyla."

"I'll fix up a mat for you to sleep on tonight," Sapphira said to Zuka.

When she left, Zuka stood alone in the courtyard. He had passed the tall tower of Shechem in his wanderings. But could it be a real home for him?

A glint of light flashed above him on the rooftop. He looked up. Taavi's knife! Was Taavi up there spying on him? What if this promise of taking him to Shechem tomorrow was just a way to keep him here for the night? Maybe tomorrow they'd turn him over to his accusers. Obviously Taavi had contacts.

The need to escape drummed through Zuka's body. There had to be a way out of this city. After all, he had freed himself from tighter places. Four tall clay jars stood against a section of the courtyard wall. He squeezed behind them.

In a few minutes, Sapphira came back. She called his name. Zuka didn't move or answer.

I Wonder . . .
I wonder if there have been times when it was hard for you to trust God . . .

Find your delight in the LORD. Then he will give you everything your heart really wants.

Psalm 37:4

On the Run Again

Zuka heard Grandfather tell Sapphira that if Zuka was telling the truth, he would have stayed around.

Just a stone's throw away, he heard Sapphira's soft cries. It would only take a whisper to call her. They could run to Shechem tonight. But could he take care of her on the way? He could barely take care of himself. It'd be selfish taking her away from what was good and safe.

Zuka heard his friend's small movements. Then she was gone.

He stretched the cramps out of his legs and moved out of his hiding place. His foot stumbled over something soft. Bending over, he discovered one of Yerick's sheep. It was Noga, the little sheep that Yerick always worried about.

Zuka picked up the bundle of black wool. Noga quivered as if she were afraid. Zuka nestled her on his shoulder just like Yerick did when one of the sheep was in trouble. Then, like the branches of a tree after the wind stopped, Noga was calm. Gently and quietly Zuka brought her over to the other sleeping sheep. "You have to be where it's safe," he whispered.

Was Shechem that safe place for him? Tomorrow might be too late. Zuka rolled his ragged robe around a loaf of bread and a goatskin of milk. Then he climbed the steps to the rooftop and lowered himself over the edge. He dropped to the ground. After rubbing his ankles to ease the pain from the long fall, he drifted into the black, dungeon-like night.

I Wonder . . .
I wonder if you can remember a time when you didn't feel safe . . .

He will answer the prayer of those who don't have anything. He won't say no to their cry for help.

Psalm 102:17

A Clear Road

When trouble
comes to them,
they will have
what they need.

Psalm 37:19a

A half-night's distance from Bethel, Zuka found a hillside cave. He crawled inside and slept for a few hours. In the morning, he tore off a chunk of bread and drank a few swallows of milk. He didn't dare finish it. It might be his only food for days.

From the cave entrance Zuka could see a winding road. He'd make better time traveling the road than climbing through the hills. It'd be worth taking the chance just to get to Shechem faster.

Once he was on the road, he noticed it was clear of boulders. And a bridge over the gully made him feel as if he had the wings of a bird.

On the other side of the bridge, a cloaked man thrust out his stick. Zuka panicked. Should he run while he still could?

"Did you have any trouble on the road?" asked the man.

"No," Zuka said, "it was smooth and peaceful."

A smile deepened the man's weathered, creased face. "The road to Shechem is my duty," he said. "I keep it clear for travelers like you."

Zuka slowly breathed in the soft afternoon air. "Thank you," he said.

"You're not there yet, though," said the old man. "You must still travel between the two mountains. Then you'll see the tower of safety."

Up ahead, Zuka saw a rocky, jagged mountain and a rounded mountain with green trees. What dangers hid behind those cliffs?

I Wonder . . .

I wonder if Psalm 37:19a would be a good verse to memorize . . .

Two Mountains

"Do evil men often hide in the rocks?" Zuka asked.

"Don't you know the story of these mountains?" the man asked.

Zuka shook his head.

"See the rounded mountain that is green with trees?" said the man. "On that mountain, God told Moses to bless all those who obeyed the law. On the opposite mountain, the one that is rocky, God cursed all those who broke the law.* So before you enter Shechem, remember there is good and evil. Think about what God sees in you."

Zuka knew he didn't kill his master, but laws about lying and stealing were from God too. What did God think of him? Maybe it wasn't Taavi he should have been worried about, or his accusers. Maybe it was God. And maybe the best choice was to turn around and spend the rest of his days hiding in caves.

"Aren't you going ahead?" asked the man.

"No," Zuka answered. "I'm afraid. God knows my sin."

The man stretched out his arms, causing his wide robe to spread from top to bottom and from fingertip to fingertip. "My robe is small. God's robe covers the earth. Forgiveness is under God's robe," he said. "Go, find out for yourself."

Zuka's heart beat fast, but his feet moved slowly. Was God watching him now? Did God see a boy who wanted to change and obey God?

I Wonder . . .
I wonder if you've ever had feelings like Zuka's . . .

*See Deuteronomy 11:26-32

God, I have heard you say two things. One is that you, God, are strong. The other is that you, Lord, are loving.

Psalm 62:11-12a

— 67 —

Shechem

Zuka kept his eyes turned toward the green mountain. He didn't notice that two men crouched on a rocky ledge of the jagged mountain. Suddenly the men jumped in front of Zuka and blocked his path.

He didn't even have to look at their faces. Immediately he recognized the showy robes of his accusers. He lifted his face to meet theirs. But before he saw their beardless chins, he felt himself being swooped up.

The cloaked arms of the man he had met earlier gripped him. The strong arms placed him on the man's shoulders—like a shepherd, rescuing a lamb. Then the man ran as if he were a horse and Zuka were the rider. They passed through double-walled gates. The gates scraped across the ground as they closed behind them.

"We made it," the man said, letting Zuka slide down. "My name is Jore. Besides being the keeper of the road, I'm an elder in Shechem. If you need protection, I'm here."

Zuka laughed while tears ran trails through his dirt-crusted face. "I never expected to be saved by being carried on someone's shoulders," he said, trying to catch his breath. Then he told the elder his story.

Jore poured soothing oil on Zuka's head and announced to all those living in Shechem that Zuka was innocent.

I Wonder . . .
I wonder how Zuka felt when Jore told the people he was innocent . . .

I find my rest in God alone. He is the One who saves me. He is like a fort to me. I will always be secure.

Psalm 62:1-2b

Isaac and Rebekah

Genesis 24

Have you ever made muffins with your mother or father? The flour and eggs that go into the batter don't look or taste like muffins. But you trust the recipe. And when you take the muffins out of the oven, you realize the recipe was right after all.

Prayers can work out that way too. Abraham gave his servant some instructions for finding a wife for Isaac. They seemed like strange ways to go about finding a wife—sort of a strange recipe for a marriage. But the servant prayed to God to show him the way, and God turned these instructions into the recipe for a good marriage. God loved Isaac and wanted to bless him with the right wife.

Psalm 69:13 reminds us that God answers prayer. Love for you is the recipe.

Litany	
Lambs	**Kids**
LORD, I pray to you.	
	Show me your favor.
LORD, I pray to you.	
	Answer me because you love me so much.
LORD, I pray to you.	
	Answer me because your love is so good.

Song for the Week
"Psalm 25," *Songs for LiFE* 50

Prayer for the Week
Lord, I trust you.
When I call to you,
you come and find me.
You give me what I need
because your plans for me are good. Amen.

One Corn Cake Short

Martha ran up the stone steps to the rooftop. She needed Aunt Zera's help. Kyla was in the sleeping room, crying, and Martha didn't know what to do or say. On the rooftop, Jensine was grinding corn. Aunt Zera was making cakes from the corn flour. They didn't seem to notice Martha.

"The baby will come in the spring," Aunt Zera said.

Jensine pounded the corn so fine that small dust clouds rose into the air.

Aunt Zera set aside another corn cake. Then she rubbed her middle. "For years I thought Yerick would be my only child. But now this baby is growing inside of me. And I have you and the little girls too. Of course you are more help than Chana and Martha."

Martha ducked behind a row of tall granary jars. What did Aunt Zera mean? Did she think seven- and eight-year-old girls were too much work?

"And Kyla?" Jensine asked. "Are you going to be her mother too?"

Martha leaned forward so she wouldn't miss what Aunt Zera had to say.

A frown crossed Aunt Zera's face. "Kyla won't be here much longer. She has tasted wickedness. In a few weeks, she'll be gone again."

Martha counted the corn cakes stacked beside Aunt Zera. There weren't enough for everyone. Had Aunt Zera purposely not made one for Kyla? If that was true, Aunt Zera was wrong. Kyla needed a mother.

I Wonder . . .
I wonder if you think that Martha is right—that Kyla needs the love of a mother . . .

The LORD takes good care of all those who fall. He lifts up all those who feel helpless.

Psalm 145:14

Shoes

Martha escaped down the steps before Aunt Zera or Jensine discovered her. She found Kyla sitting next to the short wall that surrounded the animal pen. Her matted hair covered her face. Martha took the bone comb that lay on Kyla's lap. She parted Kyla's hair down the center of her head. Then, a strand at a time, she combed through the matted black hair until it fell into smooth ripples around Kyla's face.

Martha wondered what would happen if she lowered herself onto Kyla's lap and snuggled against her? But before she could find out, Chana came skipping into the courtyard. A pair of shoes were swinging in her hand.

"Kyla," she sang, "look what I found for you."

Martha wished she was as cheery as her older sister. And that she had thought of bringing Kyla a gift.

"It's your Sabbath shoes," Chana said. "I found them at the bottom of the dry cistern. The strap was broken, so I fixed them."

Kyla reached for the shoes. "A month ago, I tossed them down there. But now I'm glad to see them." She brought Chana close and hugged her.

Martha bent over, tucking in the broken strap of her own shoe. Chana was thoughtful to give Kyla the shoes. But she'd do more for Kyla. She'd find a mother for Kyla.

I Wonder . . .
I wonder if you have ever tried to help someone who is sad . . .

The LORD is gracious. He is kind and tender. He is full of love.

Psalm 145:8

The Mother Prayer

Martha watched Kyla leave with the shoes held tightly in her hand. "Chana," said Martha, "I have an idea. Remember the story Grandfather told us about the man who wanted a wife? And the next day he found one at the market. What if we found a mother for Kyla at the market? 'Cause I don't think Aunt Zera wants Kyla."

Chana didn't say anything. It was as if she were waiting for a bird to drop the answer from the sky. "Martha," she finally said,. "you missed the part in the story where the man prayed. And the wife he found was his cousin's friend."

"We can pray," Martha said.

Chana took Martha's hand. "The market really isn't a place to find a mother."

Martha liked the comfort of Chana's hand. It seemed to untie the knots that were inside of her. If only Chana didn't act as if she was wiser because she was a year older. Sometimes it just helped to dream up answers.

"Could we still pray?" Martha asked.

"Let's go to the rooftop," Chana said, continuing to hold Martha's hand. "It's a good place to pray."

"We're sad," Martha prayed, "and lonely for Kyla. She doesn't have a mother."

After they prayed, Martha saw Aunt Hulda waving to them from two rooftops away—wonderful, loving Aunt Hulda. She would be a mother to Kyla.

I Wonder . . .
I wonder if you're thinking of someone you should pray for today . . .

The LORD is ready to help all those who call out to him.

Psalm 145:18a

The Blanket

Martha squeezed Chana's hand. "I think Aunt Hulda wants us to come over."

Chana agreed, so they ran hand in hand through the narrow path to Aunt Hulda's.

"Welcome," Aunt Hulda said, her arms wide open. "I was just thinking about you two—less than a minute before you waved to me. It's fun when things happen that way, don't you think?" Both girls nodded.

Aunt Hulda gave them chunks of fresh goat cheese. "I'll be right back," she said as the girls bit into the cheese.

Before the cheese was gone, Aunt Hulda returned with a cream-colored blanket. "Feel how soft it is," Aunt Hulda said, holding the blanket out to the girls. "I've been weaving it on the rooftop loom. I finished it just before I saw you. What do you think?"

Martha rubbed the blanket against her cheek. Then she smelled it. The blanket was full of the fresh air—it was like sun and raindrops. "It's wonderful," she said.

"You may have it," Aunt Hulda said. "I was going to sell it at the market. You never know, though, who will buy it, or if it will be appreciated or not."

The girls hugged their aunt.

"Do you suppose," Aunt Hulda said, "Kyla would like to learn how to weave? She is old enough. And I'd like to teach her."

"We'll ask her," Martha said. "Right now."

I Wonder . . .

I wonder if you know someone who is as thoughtful as Aunt Hulda . . .

You open your hand and satisfy the needs of every living creature.

Psalm 145:16

A Multiplied Answer

I will talk about the great things you have done. They will celebrate your great goodness.

Psalm 145:6b-7a

Martha and Chana wrapped themselves together in the blanket. It was hard walking that way. Their mismatched steps made them giggle.

An old woman stopped them. "Who's in there being so silly?" she asked. The girls let the blanket slip down to let her see who they were.

"I know you," the old woman said. "Every day I pray for you. You see, I grew up without a mother. At first I thought I'd always be sad, but then I found out that God never leaves a motherless or fatherless child alone. God orders the whole community to take care of them. God will watch over you. Never be afraid."

Chana kissed the old woman's fingers. Martha's heart hurt more than ever. But she didn't know why. Aunt Hulda cared about Kyla, and the old woman added her prayers. So what was wrong? Martha ran ahead of Chana into the courtyard. Kyla sat there as if she was waiting.

Kyla held out one of Martha's torn tunics. Only it wasn't torn anymore. "I fixed it," Kyla said. "When you helped me with my hair, and Chana helped me with my shoes, I knew it's good to be cared for. Now I want to take care of you and Chana. Soon I'll be twelve. I could be sort of a mother to you. If you want me."

Mother. At the sound of the word, Martha knew she was the one who wanted a mother. She ran into Kyla's arms.

I Wonder . . .

I wonder how God can know exactly what each baby, each child, each grown-up needs . . .

I wonder how you can tell that God is caring for Martha, Chana, and Kyla . . .

Jacob Steals the Blessing

Genesis 27-28:15

C an you remember a time when you lied and yet still had plenty to eat that day? Have you ever said an unkind word or thought something mean about another person, and still had the teacher praise you for your good work? If you always got what you deserved, you'd be miserable.

God knows about the real you, yet God is faithful when you call to him. Look for God's faithfulness each day. Pray and call out the words from Psalm 143:8.

Litany	
Lambs	**Kids**
In the morning let me hear about your faithful love,	
	because I've put my trust in you.
Show me the way I should live,	
	because I pray to you.

Song for the Week
"Lord, I Pray," *Songs for LiFE* 37

Prayer for the Week
Lord, I can't cover up
the wrong things that I do.
You know all about me.
But that doesn't stop you from blessing me.
Thank you for your faithful love. Amen.

Note: Before Jesus came to earth, God's people set aside the seventh day (Saturday). It was a holy day. God wanted people to rejoice over all of creation. Now Sunday is the day set aside for worshiping and praising God. It is the first day of the week—the day Christ rose from the dead. Our salvation is such a big deal, we need a day to rejoice in it.

WEEK 11

Enough?

The LORD will
certainly give
what is good.

Psalm 85:12a

All day long Joosef watched the sun move across the sky. Most of the time it seemed stuck between the hills of Ephraim. At sundown the Sabbath would begin. Grandfather had promised important Sabbath blessings. Earlier in the week, Grandfather had met the boy Samuel, who lived with Eli. Grandfather said that Samuel heard the voice of God. Now, at the age of twelve, Samuel knew his purpose for the rest of his life.

Joosef's heart rippled like stones skipping across the water. Would Grandfather's blessing from God mean that he, Joosef, son of Gersham, would also know his purpose? Perhaps there was more for him than just being the boy who limped.

The only thing that took away from his excitement was wondering about the blessings his brother and cousins would get.

Taavi would most likely get the first and best blessing because he was the oldest. Joosef wasn't much younger than Taavi, but he still wasn't second. His twin brother, Joel, was born a full song before him. His mother said she was singing a song about Joel's birth, and when she finished the song, surprise! She had another baby boy. Joosef always had the idea that she was too surprised to sing a song for him. It was as if he missed his birth blessing. Was that why one of his legs grew longer than the other?

Joosef told himself, "Be happy, be happy." A special Sabbath blessing might not make his leg grow, but something good had to come out of it.

I Wonder . . .
I wonder if you know what a blessing is . . .
I wonder if you can name some of your blessings . . .

Jacob's Blessing

Joosef sat on the stone step outside his house. A row of ants marched close to his toes. Most of them carried crumbs of bread as large as themselves. "Look at you," he said. "Who blessed you with so much?"

The great Jacob in Grandfather's stories had set up a stone pillar in Bethel long ago. He was blessed by God on that spot and he named it Bethel. Joosef felt proud to live in the town Jacob named. After he finished the chores, he'd find the pillar.

As usual, Joel was gone hunting, so Joosef would have to go by himself. He pushed away the resentment that crept into his heart over his stronger twin.

Not far from his house he found a tall stone that pointed upward. It was Jacob's pillar. Joosef sat down beside it, trying to imagine what it was like for Jacob. It must have been wonderful to dream about angels coming down from heaven. Jacob called this place holy. He said it was the gate of heaven.

Joosef looked up to the sky. If heaven's gate was above him, would God come out and see him? Suddenly that seemed scary.

He put his hand on the stone pillar, saying a promise of his own that was close to Jacob's. "May God be with me. The LORD will be my God. He will give me all that I need. I will give him a tenth of all he gives me" (Gen. 28:20-22).

Joosef looked back up into the sky. He didn't see any angels, but he believed God listened at heaven's gate.

I Wonder...
I wonder if there is something (like Jacob's pillar) in your house to remind you of God's promise to be with you . . .

You blessed the people of Jacob with great success again.

Psalm 85:1b

Off Guard

LORD, show us
your faithful love.
Save us.

Psalm 85:7

Joosef put himself into other parts of Jacob's story. He did it often enough so the story was familiar. In many ways he was like Jacob. He was the younger twin, just like Jacob. Also he was the twin that stayed home while his brother went hunting.

But there were differences too. Unlike Esau, Joel loved the blessings. He was a good brother too. The badger-skin shoes Joosef wore were a gift from Joel. So Joosef never really wanted to trick Joel out of anything. Taavi was a different story. If there was any way he could turn a blessing away from Taavi, he'd do it.

Two days ago Joosef accidentally surprised Taavi under the oak tree. Taavi was counting gold coins when Joosef limped past. Taavi quickly tried to hide the coins, but it was too late. It made Joosef wonder if the coins were stolen or earned in a dishonest way.

"Joosef."

The sound of someone calling his name took him away from his thoughts. It was Sapphira, Taavi's sister.

Joosef smiled at his little cousin Sapphira. In her simple brown dress and sun-kissed brown skin, she could be a brown bird.

"What are you doing way over here by the pillar?" he asked.

Her black eyelashes lowered to her cheeks. "Thinking about blessings," she said. "Do you think Grandfather will have a blessing for me—or will he give it all to the boys?"

I Wonder . . .
I wonder if there's any end to God's blessings for us . . .

A Trick

Joosef knew how Sapphira felt. He was worried about getting a share of the blessing too. The problem was, he didn't know how to fix it.

An ox with a rope dragging from its neck rumbled past them. "That's Taavi's new ox," Sapphira said. "He got it as a gift for helping some travelers. We'd better send it back home. Otherwise Taavi will have to go looking for it. Then he won't make it home by sundown for Sabbath."

An idea started coming to Joosef. "You go home," he said to Sapphira. "And get ready for Sabbath. I'll take care of the ox."

Sapphira ran down the path toward her house.

Joosef hurried after the ox. The ox was slow, so soon he was able to catch the rope. Easing his hand up the rope, he came face-to-face with the animal. Its eyes were large and gentle. "Nice ox," he said. "Just follow me. I'll take you to a place with tall grass—a place where Taavi will have to walk a long way to find you."

The narrow winding streets of Bethel were already empty. Joosef had to hurry. Once the sun was down, he had to be sitting at Grandfather Barzilla's table.

The ox stuck its wide nose into every little bush. Joosef brushed the sweat off his forehead. "Come on," he pleaded. "Just a little farther."

They came to a patch of grass. It wasn't the field Joosef had in mind. But the sun was level with the hilltops. Now what? If anyone met him at this late hour, they'd scold him for being out when the Sabbath was ready to begin. He had to get home fast.

I Wonder . . .
I wonder what Joosef is planning . . .

God our Savior, make us new again. Stop being unhappy with us.

Psalm 85:4a

An Empty Seat

Joosef's heart raced as he remembered a secret loose stone in Bethel's wall. All he had to do was move the stone, scramble through the hole, run around the city wall, and then back through the gate. He might make it even though he wasn't as fast as Joel.

There wasn't a trace of sun left by the time Joosef opened Grandfather's courtyard gate. Inside the house, Grandfather sat at the head of the low table. Was Grandfather thinking that one of his grandsons wasn't obedient like the boy Samuel?

Grandfather stood. He walked over to Joosef with a pitcher of water.

Trembling, Joosef held out his hands. Grandfather poured the water over Joosef's dirty hands. Hope leaped up inside of him. Clean hands were a kind of blessing—a blessing that told him God forgave and made him clean.

It was scary hobbling over to his empty place by the table. Then he thought of Taavi. He looked across the table. Taavi was there! He wasn't out searching for his ox.

Sapphira kicked him under the table. "Yerick had to whistle to make the ox come home," she whispered.

Joosef put his head down. "Never again," he thought, "will I try to mess up someone else's blessing just to get more for myself. The only blessing I want now is to be forgiven."

I Wonder . . .
I wonder if you've ever thought forgiveness is a blessing . . .

I will listen to what God the LORD will say. He promises peace to his faithful people. But they must not return to their foolish ways.

Psalm 85:8

God Blesses Jacob

Genesis 29-30:24

Imagine that your teacher gives you a lump of clay. Then she shows you how to roll the clay and how to shape it into different kinds of animals. Suddenly you are having fun and making things you never knew you could.

Having good supplies is a little bit like receiving a blessing. A blessing is more than good wishes on what you do; it is a way of giving you what you need.

Jacob's life is made rich with family and flocks of animals. All of this comes to him because of God's blessing on him.

Blessings from God are for you too. In Numbers 6:24-26 is a blessing God told Moses to pass on to the people.

Litany	
Lambs	**Kids**
May the LORD bless you	
	and take good care of you.
May the LORD smile on you	
	and be gracious to you.
May the LORD look on you with favor	
	and give you his peace.

Song for the Week
"May the Lord Bless You," *Songs for LiFE* 80

Prayer for the Week
My Lord and my God,
thank you for blessing me.
Thank you for taking care of me
and for being so good to me.
May I find peace today
because you have blessed me. Amen.

A Pond Full of Water

Joosef, Joel, and their parents spent the night at Grandfather's. In the morning, just before the sun lightened the sky, Grandfather woke Joosef.

"Come with me," Grandfather said.

Joosef rubbed his eyes. Why was Grandfather waking him up so early? The sound of Grandfather's voice told him not to question, so he rolled off his mat. Grandfather moved quickly to the animal pen. Joosef followed Grandfather's strong, wide feet.

First Grandfather untied Fifne from the post. Then, leading the donkey, they left Bethel, walking the stony path toward the stream. They stopped at the deep, glassy pool. Fifne stomped her foot in the pool.

"Do you see that?" Grandfather asked. "Fifne sees her reflection in the water and thinks another donkey is there, taking her water."

"Silly Fifne," Joosef said.

Grandfather scooped up water in his hand and offered it to Fifne. "The stream always fills this pool. If there were two donkeys or even ten, there would be enough water. It's the same way with God. God's supply is never empty."

"Last night," Joosef said, "did you find out why I was late?"

Grandfather put his arm around Joosef. "Sapphira told me. The rest was just guessing—and knowing. I was like you one time too."

I Wonder . . .
I wonder if you can say in a different way what Grandfather was teaching Joosef . . .

Give thanks to the LORD, because he is good. His faithful love continues forever.

Psalm 136:1

Blessings for Taavi, Yerick, Joel, and Joosef

On the way back to Bethel, Joosef walked beside Grandfather and Fifne.

"Do you think Fifne knows the donkey in the pool is really her?" Joosef asked.

"Not yet," Grandfather said.

Joosef chased a fly away from Fifne's ear. "I hope I won't always be such a slow learner about God's goodness," he said. "Thank you, Grandfather."

Grandfather swatted at another fly. "We need to help each other. It's inside of us to worry and to be jealous."

The sun rose like a great glowing ball. Joosef felt older and somewhat wiser walking beside Grandfather instead of behind him.

When they reached Grandfather's house, breakfast smells and noises filled the air. An extra loaf was on the table to remind them that God provides.

After breakfast, Grandfather placed his hands on Taavi's shoulders. "Make sure you obey the LORD your God completely. If you do those things, the LORD will honor you" (Deut. 28:1).

Joosef listened as Grandfather gave the same blessing to Joel and Yerick. Grandfather paused behind Joosef, then he said. "Pay attention to God's commands. Be careful to follow them. Then you will always be on top. You will never be on the bottom" (Deut. 28:13).

For the first time, Joosef knew that could be true—even for a boy with a limp.

I Wonder . . .
I wonder if you have ever been jealous of something someone else has . . .

Give thanks to the greatest God of all. His faithful love continues forever.

Psalm 136:2

Kyla's Heart

Kyla twisted the ring on her finger. Many of God's people had rings and bracelets. It was good to enjoy beautiful things. Father and Grandfather never told her she must take off the ring. Aunt Hulda admired it, saying it flattered Kyla's slim fingers.

It wasn't just a ring though. It was part of her days in the Canaanite city of Megiddo. It was part of the way she gave up her trust in God and trusted the god of Baal.

Ever since she came back to Bethel, Kyla had been sorting through differences between the Canaanites and the people of God. The Canaanites wanted to be blessed. They wanted the good things of the land—fields full of fruits and grains, barns full of wheat and barley, and cisterns full of water.

Worshiping Baal seemed to be a quicker way of getting what they wanted. After all, Baal was the god of sun and rain. Those things could be seen and touched. Also, the sacrifices Baal demanded were easier than waiting for God. Who could be like Abraham, Isaac, or Jacob, who waited years for God's promises? Who could give their heart and trust to God when they wanted rain tomorrow?

Kyla looked at the table of food that was blessed by goodness. Joy was in the room and in the hearts of all of her cousins and family. Every Sabbath celebrated God's creation of the world and the gifts that filled the earth. Baal wasn't a creator like the Lord God. If Baal created anything, it was greed and selfishness.

I Wonder . . .
I wonder if you can name some blessings you can see and touch . . .
I wonder if you can name some blessings you can't see and touch . . .

Give thanks to the most powerful Lord of all. His faithful love continues forever.

Psalm 136:3

Kyla's Blessing

Kyla twisted the ring all the way off. She dropped it on the ground. "Lord God," she prayed, "I want to trust you. Forgive me for turning against your command not to have any other gods. Help me when I find it hard to trust you. Amen."

She sensed Grandfather's presence behind her. He put his hand on her head. It was as if he was blessing the prayer she had prayed in her mind.

"Kyla," he said, his voice kind and gentle. "Do you have a thread?"

Taavi, who was sitting across from Kyla, mumbled, "Grandfather is asking her for a thread because he doesn't have a blessing for her. Watch and see, he'll give her work."

No one seemed to hear Taavi or pay attention to him. But Kyla heard. Her head dropped to her chest.

Grandfather's hand went under her chin, gently lifting it up. "When I thought about Kyla," he said to everyone, "I saw the picture of her mending her sister's clothes."

Kyla unpinned the needle and thread from her tunic. She gave it to Grandfather.

He held it up, slipping his fingers over the thread and stopping at the knot. "There was always a thread connecting Kyla to us," he said. "The thread was prayer. And God provided the knot at the end. It stopped her from leaving us altogether."

Again Grandfather placed his hand on Kyla's head. "The LORD your God will make you his holy people. He will set you apart for himself" (Deut. 28:9a).

I Wonder . . .
I wonder how Kyla felt when she heard Grandfather's blessing . . .

He set us free
from our enemies.
His faithful love
continues forever.

Psalm 136:24

Blessings for Jensine, Chana, Martha, and Sapphira

Sapphira loved clapping, dancing, and all sorts of joyful noise made in praise of God. Today, though, the blessings filled her with great silence. It was as if God was in the silence. Perhaps Abraham, Isaac, Jacob, and Moses were shouting praises to God. Those four great men of God were like the four corners that held up everything.

Silence also held her as she wondered when it would be her turn. She wasn't next. Grandfather stopped at Kyla's sisters. He gathered the three girls in his arms. "My beautiful granddaughters," he said. "May you be blessed with the beauty of Sarah, Rebekah, and Rachel." Jensine, Chana, and Martha each gave Grandfather a kiss.

Sapphira knew the beauty he blessed the girls with was not just beauty of the outside; it was a beauty of the inside too—a beauty that came from trusting God. So why didn't Grandfather include her in that blessing?

Grandfather paused as if he were finished. Sapphira hardly let herself blink. She didn't want anyone to notice her if Grandfather had missed or forgotten her.

Then, moving like honey out of a jar, Grandfather went over to Sapphira. He said, "The LORD will give you more than you need" (Deut. 28:11a).

"It's time to celebrate," Grandmother said. "Let's eat."

In less time than it took to milk a goat, the table overflowed with bread, honey, olives, cheese, and figs. Grandmother always hid the best food until Sabbath.

I Wonder . . .
I wonder if God has given *you* more than you need . . .

Give thanks to the One who remembered us when things were going badly for us. His faithful love continues forever. Give thanks to the God of heaven. His faithful love continues forever.

Psalm 136:23, 26

Jacob Meets Esau

Genesis 32:1-21; 33

W hen Jacob and Esau left each other, they were enemies. Even many years later, Jacob was afraid of meeting Esau. He prepared gifts for Esau; then he prayed. In his prayer, Jacob remembered all that God had given him. He knew his strength came from God—and that there was strength enough to offer peace to Esau.

Call on God's strength as you echo the words from Psalm 59:9, 17.

Litany	
Lambs	**Kids**
You give me strength.	
	You are my loving God.
God, you are like a fort to me.	
	You are my loving God.
You give me strength.	
	You are my loving God.

Song for the Week
"I Will Sing, I Will Sing," *Songs for LiFE* 8, stanzas 1, 3

Prayer for the Week
When I need to be strong,
Lord, I call to you.
When I am strong,
Lord, I thank you. Amen.

Divided Land

Taavi jabbed his wooden plow through the center of a new green wheat sprout. He didn't care. For weeks he had been working the new strip of land on the hillside. The land belonged to his father and uncles, but even so, he dreamed that it was really his.

Then Grandfather gave half the hillside land to Joel. True, he gave the other half to Taavi, but in Taavi's mind his dream was taken from him. It'd be better to have none of it than half of it. Besides, what did Joel know about plowing the land, planting the grain, and making tunnels for water to flow down the hillside?

Joel came up the hill. He carried his bow and arrow.

"You can't weed the fields with an arrow," Taavi said to Joel.

Joel put down his hunting gear. "Grandfather's ox is for me to use too."

Taavi unhooked the plow. "Yeah, but this part belongs to me. You're not going to get rid of any weeds walking an ox through the field without a plow."

Joel was silent.

This was the moment Taavi was waiting for. "I'll do this for you," Taavi said. "Give me a piece of your land, and I'll share my plow with you." He held it out to Joel. "Without a plow you can't work any of your land. But take my deal, and someday you may earn enough grain to trade back for your land."

Joel scratched a place in the dirt, but Taavi knew he had his cousin trapped. After a handshake, Taavi piled two stones on top of each other to mark the new boundary.

I Wonder . . .
I wonder if you think Taavi's deal is fair to Joel . . .

Don't be wise in your own eyes. Have respect for the LORD and avoid evil.

Proverbs 3:7

A Plow for Joel

Taavi laughed as Joel tried to hook the wooden plow back up to the ox. Before he finished laughing, Sapphira came, dragging something behind her.

"Joel," she called out. "Look what I have for you. It's a plow with a hard metal point."

Joel dropped the reins of the ox. "Where did you get it?"

"From Grandfather's blessing."

Taavi thought about Sapphira's blessing. Grandfather said she'd get more than she needed. But it turned out to be nothing. Unlike Yerick and Joosef, who received sheep, Sapphira just went along on visits with Grandfather to his friends.

"It's an iron plow point," Sapphira said. "The best kind. Every one of Grandfather's friends had a gift for me. When I got this gift, I thought of you, Joel."

Taavi couldn't stand to listen to anymore. He decided he had only one choice and that was to leave. Why should he stay around the hills of Bethel any longer? Everyone was against him. Grandfather had no right to make owning a field so easy for Joel. Sapphira should have thought of her brother before she gave a gift to her cousin.

He threw his plow down in front of Joel. "Here, take my plow too. You take everything else." Then he ran.

"Taavi, where are you going?" Sapphira called as she ran after him.

I Wonder . . .
I wonder if you have ever been jealous of someone . . .

Honor the LORD with your wealth.

Proverbs 3:9

Taavi Runs

Taavi stopped to shout back at Sapphira. "The Midianites who owned Zuka cared more about me than anyone in my family. Maybe I'll find them."

"No, Taavi, you can't. You belong to a covenant God. When God made promises to Abraham, Isaac, Jacob, and Moses, those promises were made to you too."

Taavi stood still. His beating heart lifted his chest up and down. "I don't feel the promises," he shouted back at her. Then he ran again. Higher and higher into the hills he went. The sky darkened. Every breath he took hurt. He had to rest. But he wasn't going to give up. He could take care of himself and find a new life for himself.

Tonight he'd sleep against a rock. In the morning, he'd start out again.

An owl hooted in a nearby tree under a moonless sky. The grass beside him rustled. Mice! He climbed on top of the rock, trying his best to get comfortable.

The next morning a cloud of dust rose from the road below. It was a large caravan with camels. Quickly Taavi zigzagged down the hill.

The nose rings on the camels and their brightly colored blankets excited him. A man from the caravan approached him. "Aren't you far away from home?" he asked.

"I don't have a home," Taavi answered.

The man moved closer until his breath was hot on Taavi. Grease and dirt stains on his tunic mixed with sweat. "We're getting ready to eat," said the man. "You hungry?"

I Wonder . . .
I wonder when you can "feel" God's promises . . .
I wonder when it's hard to feel them . . .

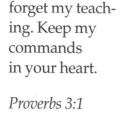

My son, do not forget my teaching. Keep my commands in your heart.

Proverbs 3:1

On the Road

At the mention of eating, Taavi knew he was hungrier than he had ever been.

He followed the man to the side of the road. The rest of the caravan people had set up a temporary camp. They started a fire. Then someone lifted a blanket off the bulging side of a camel. An animal carcass was under the blanket. A man whipped out a knife and hacked off a piece of raw meat.

Taavi had never seen a dead pig's body before. Curiosity forced him over to the carcass. Small white worms crawled over the dead animal.

Several reed lengths from him, the meat was being roasted over the fire. A mixture of disgust and hunger gnawed at Taavi. God's laws were very strict about food. Pigs were forbidden; they were unclean. Taavi thought he'd vomit from his empty stomach. But he didn't; he ran and didn't look back.

Clouds filled the noon sky. Taavi's heart lifted in thankfulness for the promise of rain. It was just what the wheat and barley fields needed. Wait—why was he concerned about the land? Sapphira was right. He was connected to the land—to the goodness of the Lord. If only he could have another chance!

A distant pounding came up through the ground. Taavi stepped aside as a chariot sped past him. It was as fast as a lion in a chase. Then unexpectedly it stopped and turned around, coming to a full stop beside him.

I Wonder . . .
In the days before refrigerators and food inspectors, God instructed the people what to eat and what not to eat. I wonder what God thinks is bad for us or good for us today . . .

The LORD trains those he loves.

Proverbs 3:12

Taavi Returns

A man dressed in wealthy robes leaned over the side of the chariot. "May I take you somewhere?" he asked.

Taavi trembled with fear and joy. "I want to go home—to Bethel—to my family and my land."

The man narrowed his eyes as if he were inspecting Taavi. "Climb aboard," he said, ordering Taavi into the chariot. The man told the driver to go to Bethel, and Taavi relaxed. In less time that it took to plow a field, they were at Bethel.

As Taavi moved to the chariot door, the man grabbed Taavi by the arm. "Not so fast. You owe me a homer of barley from your land. This ride wasn't for free."

"But the fields aren't ripe yet," Taavi said.

"I'll be back to collect in the spring." The man's lips curled. "If you don't have it, I'll take *you*."

Taavi knew he was trapped. Was this how he made Joel feel?

"Would you take a plow?" Taavi asked, in a voice just above a whisper.

The man agreed. And as Taavi ran to get it, he remembered Grandfather's blessing. "Make sure you obey the LORD your God completely. If you do these things, the LORD will honor you." From his greed over the land to his cold heart toward God and his family, Taavi had disobeyed. He handed the chariot driver the wooden plow. Then, falling down on his knees, Taavi bowed his head.

I Wonder . . .
I wonder what Taavi will say to God . . .
To Grandfather . . .
To Joel and Sapphira . . .

Blessed is the one who finds wisdom. Blessed is the one who gains understanding.

Proverbs 3:13

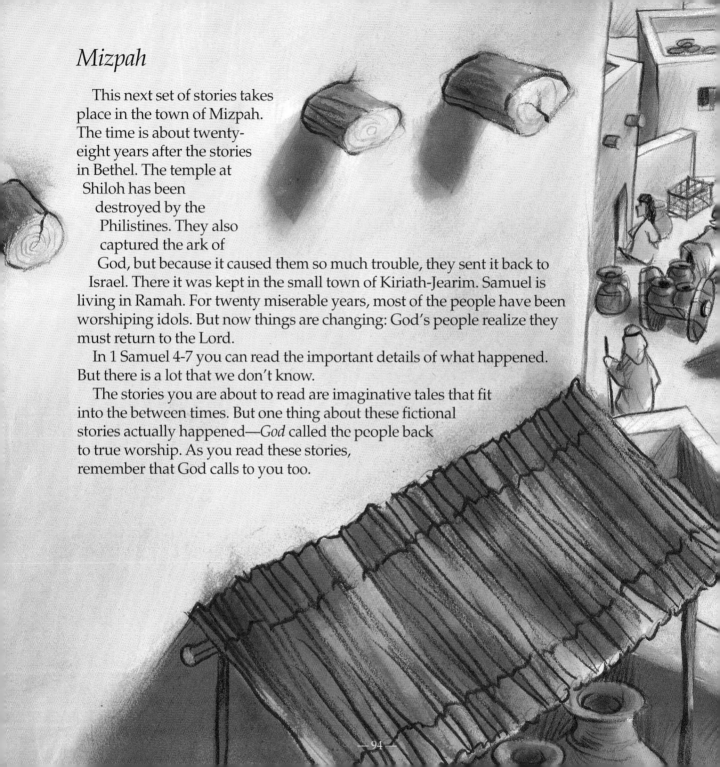

Mizpah

This next set of stories takes place in the town of Mizpah. The time is about twenty-eight years after the stories in Bethel. The temple at Shiloh has been destroyed by the Philistines. They also captured the ark of God, but because it caused them so much trouble, they sent it back to Israel. There it was kept in the small town of Kiriath-Jearim. Samuel is living in Ramah. For twenty miserable years, most of the people have been worshiping idols. But now things are changing: God's people realize they must return to the Lord.

In 1 Samuel 4-7 you can read the important details of what happened. But there is a lot that we don't know.

The stories you are about to read are imaginative tales that fit into the between times. But one thing about these fictional stories actually happened—*God* called the people back to true worship. As you read these stories, remember that God calls to you too.

Rooftop Kids of Mizpah

The families in these stories live with Jerusha, a woman who lost her husband and sons in a battle against the Philistines. And since Zared, Atalie, Lily, and Ezechiel lost their home and parents in the same battle, Jerusha brought them to her home. Their husbands, wives, and children came with them.

Talori (10)
She is the only child of her father, Zared. Her mother died when Talori was born. She wants to be a spy, the same as her father. She is a fast runner.

Izaak (12)
He is the oldest of the cousins. He considers himself a leader for his younger cousins and brother, Shaul. He hunts wild animals. He makes clothing from the skins of the animals and various things from their bones   .

Shaul (9)
He likes to please others, especially his brother, Izaak, and his cousin Jud. He admires these older boys. He wants to be brave, and he'd like to be the best arrow maker.

Jud (11)
He helps his father make swords, daggers, arrow tips, and bronze shields. But his heart is often hard against his family and God.

Chiram (10)
The brother of Jud and Eben, who was stolen from Mizpah when he was a baby, before Eben was born. Even though his mother has not seen her middle son since the day he was stolen, she keeps track of his age. He would be ten years old. Every day she thinks about him and wonders if he is still alive.

Eben (9)

He treasures a dove feather that he found. All the animals and birds of creation are special to him. His heart longs for God.

Csilla (9)

She likes to be the center of attention. She is proud of the baskets she makes and sells in the market.

Mikele (7)

She wants to be the same as her older sister Csilla. She is learning basket-weaving from Csilla.

Chike (10)

He is the oldest son of the Philistine Lord of Ashdod. But he is not treated as the heir to the throne—that honor goes to Hapu. Chike has to figure out the mystery of his birth and his rank as second son.

   When he does, he leaves Ashdod and returns to his Israelite home.

Hapu (9)

He is the second son of the Philistine Lord of Ashdod. But he is clearly the favorite. And he becomes the young lord when his father dies.

Rinnah (8)

She is an orphan girl who roams the streets of Mizpah. She begs for food and sleeps in the corner of a broken-down stone house.

Joseph the Dreamer

Genesis 37; 39:1-6

Have you ever been in trouble? Do you remember how you felt? Do you remember what you did?

Joseph was in terrible trouble after his brothers sold him as a slave. He was away from his family in a strange place. He had no friends to talk to, no parents to turn to. But do you know what he did? He kept trusting and obeying God. And God took care of him—even far away from home in the house of Potiphar.

This week use the words of Psalm 142:1-2 to remind yourself that the Lord is there for you—no matter how much trouble you face.

Litany	
Lambs	**Kids**
I call out to the LORD.	
	I pray to him for his favor.
I call out to the LORD.	
	I pour out my problem to him.
I call out to the LORD.	
	I tell him about my trouble.

Song for the Week
"Kum Ba Yah," *Songs for LiFE* 53

Prayer for the Week
Lord, sometimes troubles are big
and sometimes they are small.
But you always have the right
amount of help and love for all.
Thank you. Amen.

A Creator God?

Eben brushed the feather of a white dove against his cheek. Then he put the feather in his carrying pouch.

Jud stood in the courtyard of their home in Mizpah, tapping his foot. "Hurry up," he yelled at Eben. "Father needs us to gather wood in the hills. Then he can keep the fire going all day in the copper furnaces. There's lots of copper to melt for arrow tips."

"Go ahead," Eben said. "I'll catch up."

"Father says I can't leave without you. Mother worries a Philistine will snatch up her big baby." Jud kicked against a tall clay jar. "I'm waiting. If Father didn't need you to carry a load of wood, I wouldn't take you."

Eben reached his hand into his pouch and stroked his fingers against the barbs of the feather. He hated worrying about making weapons all of the time. Couldn't they spend one day not thinking about their enemies, the Philistines?

After another scolding he followed Jud. They walked the ring path alongside the Mizpah wall. When they reached the town gate, Jud pulled an arrow out of his pouch. There never was a time when Jud didn't prepare himself with a weapon.

Once outside the town walls, Jud scanned the hills above them. Then he took off and Eben followed. He avoided the stones scattered on the ground. They looked as if they had fallen from the sky. Was that the way it was with people too? Did they just drop down from above to live in places where they were miserable? There had to be a better way to live. Always looking over your shoulder for an enemy was like living in a trap.

On a sunny, blue-sky morning like this one, he wanted to be alone in the hills—listening to the wind whisper and the birds tell who made them. He wanted to hear that a great God made everything and cared about nine-year-old boys.

"Is there a creator god?" he called ahead to Jud.

Jud stopped on the path. A scowl was on his face. "Don't go asking about that again. There is no way one god could do everything. A god like that would have to be greater than iron."

I Wonder . . .
I wonder how you would answer Eben's question . . .

All of the gods of the nations are like their statues. They can't do anything. But the LORD made the heavens.

Psalm 96:5

A Find

Eben watched Jud take off without looking back once to see if his younger brother was following. The question about a creator god had angered Jud. Eben guessed that he was on his own, no matter what the family rules were.

His heart beat wildly. This was his chance. He had never traveled in the hills by himself. Would he lose his way? The ridges on the west were not quite as steep as the hills Jud climbed. He went toward the low hills. Dark spots dotted the sides of the rocky ridges. Caves! He climbed until he reached the widest dark-holed entrance. Dropping to his knees, he crawled into the opening. Soon he was in a tall, narrow room. A beam of dusty light came from a hole in the ceiling. Either this was a safe place or a trap.

His searching hand touched something sharp. He focused on the object, allowing his eyes to adjust. It was a farmer's plow. Who did it belong to? He carried it to the beam of light. It was heavier than any other plow he had handled. From the weight and color of the metal tip, he decided that part was made of iron. It could mean that it belonged to a Philistine, but Eben wanted to believe the owner was a special Israelite. He ran his fingers over the wooden form above the tip. Something seemed to be carved into the wood. He traced the design with his fingers. It reminded him of a vine covered with grapes. It seemed to tell the story of grapes and things that grew, not war. He closed his eyes and imagined a boy not too much different than himself. This boy loved peace. He loved things that grew. And he knew the one and only true God, the creator God. Suddenly Eben's vision became real in his mind. Wouldn't it be wonderful to find the owner? Perhaps the owner knew about the God of the heavens who gave life.

I Wonder . . .
I wonder if there is anyone who tells you about God in heaven . . .

LORD, be good to me as you have promised. Increase my knowledge and give me good sense.

Psalm 119:65-66a

Two Visions

Don't let me lose
all hope. Take
good care of me,
and I will be
saved.

Psalm 119:116b-117

Eben carried the plow out of the cave. In the sunlight he was more convinced than before that the tip was iron and the carving was of a grapevine loaded with grapes.

And his vision of a boy using this plowshare became stronger than before. He saw a tall, tanned boy who wasn't afraid to be working in the open fields. This boy trusted God to bless his work in the fields and protect him from harm. If only the boy would appear and tell him this was all true.

But it wasn't the boy who came to him. It was Jud.

"What do you have?" Jud asked.

"I think it's a plow—one with an iron tip."

Jud dropped his stash of wood. He grabbed the plowshare out of Eben's hands. "Well, little brother, you may be of some use after all. The Philistines have prevented us from getting iron for our swords. But this little piece will melt down to make a strong dagger."

Eben gasped. "But I had a vision. I—I think this plowshare comes from a time of peace—a time when the great God blessed our people. It was when we didn't need the gods of the Canaanites and Philistines."

Jud laughed. "What do you know about gods? You're a dreamer. When you are as old as me you'll understand."

As Jud tugged at the plow in Eben's hands, the iron tip broke off the wooden form. Jud ran away with the iron part.

I Wonder . . .

I wonder if someone is ever too young to understand God . . .

Snatched Back

Eben stared at the cracked wooden pieces in his hands. When Jud tore off the iron tip the old wood split in two. The carving of the vine was ruined. Carefully Eben placed the wooden pieces under a pine tree. He had to save the iron tip before Jud melted it.

Eben pumped his short legs up and down as fast as possible. From the inner side of Mizpah's wall, smoke rose above the area of the copper-melting furnace. Hopefully the melting pots in the furnace would already be full before Jud got there. Eben sped through the gate area and dashed to the furnace. Father fanned air down the pipe leading to the hot coals. Jud stood beside Father with the iron tip, waiting.

Father spoke to Jud as Eben arrived.

"The fire needs more fuel," Father said. "Where is it?"

"I left it outside the wall," Jud said. "But Father, look what I have. Iron!"

Father took the piece from Jud. "This is solid. But we can't do anything with it if our fire is out. Go get the wood."

Jud ignored Eben on the way out.

The smoke from the oven changed to a bluish color. "The copper in the oven is melted and ready to pour," Father said, setting the plow point on the ground.

As Father readied the molds for arrow tips, Eben picked up the iron piece. Then he ran with it. He ran to a low trench on the opposite side of the town. With the iron close to his chest, he settled into the lowest part of the trench. Had he done the right thing? The iron was no better than an idol. It couldn't teach him about God. Yet he couldn't forget about the vision of the boy. "Lord God," he whispered, "will I ever learn about you?"

I Wonder . . .

I wonder if you can remember a time when you learned about God . . .

LORD, may you hear my cry. Give me understanding, just as you said you would.

Psalm 119:169

On the Run

Eben lay faceup in the trench. The clouds scurried across the sky as if they were in a hurry to go somewhere. He thought about where he could go if he left Mizpah. Last month Uncle Zared mentioned someone named Samuel. He said Samuel taught that there was only one true God. Some of his uncles and aunts laughed as if Samuel was a fool. The subject angered his father. Eben didn't dare ask questions. But day after day the questions never left his mind.

He did find out that Samuel lived in Ramah. And he did ask Uncle Zared enough questions to learn that Ramah was the next town to the north on the main road.

A flock of birds flew above him. They were free to go to Ramah. He remembered the feather in his pouch. Then he knew he had to go too. He crawled out of the trench.

By now the clouds had backed into each other and had darkened. Large single drops fell. Then streams of drops came like thousands of arrows. The rain sent everyone running for protection.

As Eben looked across the town, he was the only one in the open. Even the guard at the gate had taken cover. Eben whispered goodbye to his mother and father. As he ran, the rain washed the tears from his face and the dust from his tunic. He felt as if he were a new person. The God who sent the rain would protect him. Up ahead were the caves—a place to keep dry and safe until the rain stopped.

But when he stepped into the cave nearest the road, he sensed he was not alone. A figure approached him, holding a lighted clay-jar torch. It was a boy no older than he was. But the boy's painted chest, armbands, and fringed headgear told Eben he was sharing this cave with a Philistine.

I Wonder . . .
I wonder if you would be afraid if you were Eben . . .
I wonder what you do when you are afraid . . .

You are my place of safety. You are like a shield that keeps me safe. I have put my hope in your word.

Psalm 119:114

Joseph the Slave

Genesis 39:6-41:45

I f your classmates walked ahead of you, talking and laughing, would you feel left out? Or if you were last to be chosen for kickball, would it seem as if no one wanted you? How would your feelings change if one friend came to be with you?

When Joseph was in prison, he didn't know if he'd ever get out. But Joseph knew the kindness of God while he was there. He never had to think he was alone.

God wants you to know you don't have to be alone either. Echo the words of Psalm 54:4 and 55:22 this week. Remember these words when you feel left out and lonely.

Litany	
Lambs	**Kids**
I know that God helps me.	
	The Lord is the one who keeps me going.
Turn your worries over to the LORD.	
	He will keep you going.

Song for the Week
"Everywhere I Go," *Songs for LiFE* 211

Prayer for the Week
Lord, being alone and scared
can happen to me on the playground.
It can happen when I'm at home.
It can happen when I'm sick.
Thank you for letting me know
you were with Joseph in prison,
so I can know you are with me everywhere. Amen.

Traded

Eben flinched as the Philistine boy raised an iron knife with a carved handle.

The Philistine grinned. But Eben didn't think it was a grin of friendship, even though the boy appeared to be Eben's age. It was a grin of triumph. One that came with victory.

The boy thrust his knife against Eben's stomach. "Hapu rules," he said. "You are my first prisoner. Great honor will come to me."

Eben guessed that with Hapu's great honor, great pain awaited his prisoner. But he wasn't as frightened as he had always imagined he might be.

A warlike cry echoed outside the caves. Eben recognized the shouting voices. It was Jud and his cousins Izaak and Shaul. Were they coming to rescue him?

"I still got you," Hapu said, holding his knife against Eben's stomach and forcing him out of the cave. The rain had stopped. The air smelled fresh and clean, but there was no time to think about that.

Jud, Izaak, and Shaul leaped over the ridge to the cave entrance, their bows aimed.

Hapu spoke as if he were the one in charge. "Welcome. I am the great Hapu, son of the lord of Ashdod. Do I have someone you want?"

"Depends," Jud said. "What are your plans?"

"I'll give him up, if you give me your bows and arrows," Hapu said.

Now Jud grinned. Then he whispered to Izaak and Shaul before speaking to Hapu. "How about if you give us your knife, and you can keep the prisoner?"

I Wonder . . .
I wonder how Eben felt when his brother offered to sell him for a knife . . .

When I am afraid,
I will trust in you.

Psalm 56:3

A Tear Stain

Eben hardly noticed the release of Hapu's knife. All he could think of were his brother's words. It was as if an arrow pierced his heart.

"It must be a trick," Hapu said. "Why else would you give him up for a knife?"

Jud stepped forward. "Look at my brother. He isn't worth much to us. He carries no weapons. He doesn't know how to fight. All you can find on him is a piece of iron. It belongs to me. I'd like it back, but I'd like your knife even more."

Hapu leaned his head to the side as if to get a better look at Eben. Then he turned back to Jud. "*You* might be against him, but what about his mother and father?"

Eben jerked his head up. Hapu understood the love of a mother and father. Did Hapu have parents who loved him? So often his own mother whispered in his ear. "You are my son," she said. "The Philistines will never take you." And his father never let him walk alone. His parents still remembered a time before Eben was born—a time when a Philistine warrior snached away Mother's second baby boy—Chiram. He was a brother Eben never had a chance to know.

Jud stumbled over some words about Mother and Father. "They'll be glad," he said, avoiding looking in Eben's direction.

Hapu handed the iron knife to Jud.

Eben's eyes blurred. He couldn't fly away and be safe like a rock dove after all. Who would save him?

I Wonder . . .
I wonder if God feels great sadness when brothers (or sisters) hurt each other . . .

"I wish I had wings like a dove! Then I would fly away and be at rest. I would escape to a place far away."

Psalm 55:6-7a

The Journey

Eben was alone with Hapu now.

"What will you do without your knife?" Eben asked.

Hapu shrugged. "You think that was my only weapon?" He stooped down, picking up a spear from the ground and pointing it at Eben. "Now go."

Eben's eyes blurred again. He couldn't think. He stumbled forward with the spear point pressing against his back.

Up ahead, the sun reflected bright beams off a chariot. "That's mine," Hapu said. "Now that the rain has stopped, my horses will take us back to Ashdod."

Eben nodded. Surely Father would come after him. If there was a Lord of the heavens, couldn't that God save him from the Philistines? He climbed into the chariot. Hapu stood and whipped the horses to move. A wild look came over Hapu as he whipped the horses to go faster and faster. This picture of Hapu was more frightening than the grinning Hapu. Eben wondered how far it was to Ashdod, but he didn't dare speak.

For the rest of the day they raced the sun. The air grew cooler, and the breeze carried smells new to Eben. Then, in the distance, he saw the red ball of the sun resting on water so wide and long that there was no end to it.

Hapu slowed the horses. He pointed to a pillared city. "That's Ashdod," he said. "And beyond that is the sea."

Eben gripped the pouch that held the iron plow point. Perhaps it would help him in some way. He must be careful to hold on to it.

I Wonder . . .

I wonder if it would help Eben to know the words of Psalm 56:11 . . .

I trust in God.
I will not be
afraid. What can
mere men do
to me?

Psalm 56:11

A Prisoner

The horses pulled the chariot through wide city gates. Eben forced his fingers loose from the tight grip around the side bars of the chariot. The broad stone paved streets and the tall pillared houses of Ashdod surprised him.

Hapu climbed out of the chariot. He mounted the horses, one foot balanced on each horse. In a loud voice he called out, "Prisoner."

Soldiers prepared to shoot their arrows came running. Four soldiers grabbed Eben, each one with a pincher hold on Eben's arms and legs. They carried him so that he faced the ground.

Eben clutched his pouch. "Please," he begged the God he hoped was in heaven, "don't let me die until I know you are the true God."

He gasped for breath as the soldiers carried him down crooked stone steps. Once the soldiers dipped so low that his nose scraped the rough stones. At the bottom, they shoved aside a large stone and dumped Eben into a dungeon. It smelled worse than a pit of dead rats. The only sign of life was the last beam of sunlight coming through a crack. Then something moved in the beam, and Eben realized he was not alone.

A bony hand crossed the beam of light. "The Lord has brought you here," said a wispy voice. "I had a dream about a boy who found the plow point belonging to me and my cousin. Could it be you?"

Eben pushed his pouch behind him.

I Wonder . . .
I wonder if God can be in dark and scary places . . .
I wonder how you can know God is there when you are in trouble . . .

My enemies will turn back when I call out to you for help. Then I will know that God is on my side.

Psalm 56:9

Taavi Prays

You have saved me from death. You have kept me from tripping and falling. Now I can live with you in the light that leads to life.

Psalm 56:13

Eben moved away from the man. Was it all a trick? Had someone told this strange man what was in the pouch?

"I'm sorry to frighten you," the man said. "My name is Taavi. What is yours?"

The kindness in Taavi's voice comforted Eben. He edged a bit closer to the man. "My name is Eben. But I'm not a Philistine. I'm an Israelite."

Taavi rocked in the disappearing light. "Yes," he finally said. "So am I."

Eben was afraid to ask Taavi how long he had been in this dungeon.

Taavi stretched out his arm to the black space. "It's sundown," he said. "Do you want to pray with me?"

Eben strained his eyes, looking for an idol in the dungeon. There wasn't one.

Taavi kneeled—his head lifted up. "Lord God of heaven and earth," Taavi prayed, "God of Israel, hear the prayer of your servant. Deliver us as you delivered Joseph. Thank you for life today, and thank you for saving the life of Eben."

Taavi was quiet after his prayer. There was sadness in his voice when he spoke. "You didn't bow in prayer with me. Do you worship the Lord?"

Eben trembled. "I wasn't sure the Lord could be down here."

"God never leaves those who trust in the name of the Lord." Taavi's voice was strong. "Rest now. We'll talk more in the morning."

Eben felt the hardness of the plow point under the cloth of the pouch. Taavi had just spoken of the God of heaven, just as the boy from his dream in the cave had spoken of God. But it was impossible for this skeleton of a person to have a connection to the tanned boy and an iron plow point.

I Wonder . . .
I wonder if you noticed that Taavi's prayer had "thank you"s in it . . .

Joseph the Governor

Genesis 41:46-46:34

Have you ever had three or more things go wrong in one day? When that happens, you might want to go to your room and pound the pillow. But while you're pounding, stop and think. Remember that even on really terrible days, you are not alone. The God who comforts and guides is there with you. And God can use even bad days to teach you great things—just as God did for Joseph. When you are wondering about the troubles you are having, remember the words from Jeremiah 29:11, 13.

Litany	
Lambs	**Kids**
"I know the plans I have for you," announces the LORD.	
	"I want you to enjoy success. I do not plan to harm you. I will give you hope."
"When you look for me with all your heart,	
	you will find me."

Song for the Week
"Lord, I Pray," *Songs for LiFE* 37

Prayer for the Week
Lord, in my troubles guide me.
Teach me and change me.
Help me find you. Amen.

Taavi's Story

Morning light streaked through the narrow slit at the dungeon entrance. Eben saw Taavi on his knees again, thanking the Lord in heaven for the light. Didn't this old prisoner know that the skinny thread of light was nothing? Worse yet, the light was cruel, showing Taavi's bones trapped in a thin layer of skin.

Eben pinched his arm. There was plenty of body between his skin and bones. How long would it take to lose it all?

After his prayers, Taavi crawled over to Eben. "Last night you must have thought I was crazy, talking about the plow point in your pouch. But to keep hope alive, I have a dream. . . . In this dream a young Israelite boy finds the plow point that belonged to me long ago."

Eben leaned back, allowing the sharp piece of iron to press against his back. "How could a farmer's tool be so important?"

Taavi took a deep breath. "Years ago, I tricked my cousin out of a simple wooden plow. Then God changed my proud, selfish heart. But instead of getting back at me, my cousin shared his iron plow point with me. From that time on, the iron plow meant God's forgiveness and blessing."

"What happened to it?" Eben asked.

"When the Philistines battled our people, I hid it in a cave near Mizpah. Later the Philistines captured me and threw me down here. An escape was more than I could hope for—that's why my prayers and dreams were for a young boy like you."

Eben couldn't speak. He was beginning to understand that he hadn't landed in this dark, cramped dungeon by mistake. And that there was a plan larger than the sky, sea, and earth.

I Wonder . . .
I wonder if God's plans for you are bigger than you can imagine . . .

"I know the plans I have for you," announces the LORD.

Jeremiah 29:11a

Trust and Thanksgiving

Eben touched the top of Taavi's hand. "Is it God who gave you the dream?"

The old man's bony frame trembled under Eben's fingers. Then Taavi's sunken eyes sparked with a bit of life. "Yes, young Eben. The God of our people, the Israelites."

"We have many gods," Eben said, his voice dropping low.

"You don't believe that, do you?" Taavi asked.

Eben reached behind him and brought the pouch to his lap. "I have your plow point, Taavi. Last night I thought you were part of a Philistine plan to trick me. But the Philistines aren't smart enough to know hidden things like what is in our dreams." He gave the plow point to Taavi.

"This is it," Taavi whispered. "God will bless us again. God will bless you, Eben."

Eben brought his knees close to his chest. The words of the blessing didn't match living the rest of his life in a dungeon. How would he ever get over being scared?

The scraping sound of rock against rock filled the dungeon. A wider streak of light cut into the darkness. Two chunks of bread rattled across the floor. Eben picked up a piece. It was too hard too eat. He threw it down again. Taavi placed the other piece on his lap and bowed his head. When he lifted his head, he tore off a bite-sized section and tossed it across the dungeon. Then, as if in answer to Eben's puzzled look, he said, "I have a mouse friend who shares my blessings. It helps me to be thankful for all that I have."

Thankful? Eben wondered. It was frightening being a prisoner, but yes, he was thankful too. He was alive. And there was something wonderful about all that had happened. He reached for his bread and gave thanks to Taavi's God.

I Wonder . . .
I wonder if you could give thanks to God in a prison or a dungeon . . .

> "I want you to enjoy success. I do not plan to harm you."
>
> *Jeremiah 29:11b*

The Golden Box

[God says,] "You will come and pray to me. And I will listen to you."

Jeremiah 29:12

Before Eben finished his bread, the mouse came to claim his share. At first Eben didn't see the small gray creature in the gray dungeon light. But there were no other sounds to cover up the mouse's scratching and eating sounds.

"The guards left me alone because of my mouse friend," Taavi said. "It saved my life."

Eben laughed. "The Philistines are afraid of mice?"

"Don't you know the story of the ark of the Lord?" Taavi asked.

Eben tossed his last bit of bread to the mouse. "I don't even know what an ark is."

Taavi rocked slowly in place. Then he began the story. "The ark is a golden box. Two cherubim sit on the top of it. And inside . . . " Taavi's voice trembled. "Inside are two tablets of stone. The words God spoke to our people are on those tablets."

Eben couldn't believe that God's box was golden and he couldn't believe that God spoke to people. Before he could decide which question to ask, Taavi took Eben's hand and moved Eben's fingers along the wall. "Feel the scratch lines on the stones," Taavi said. "The lines tell me it has been twenty years since the day the Philistines stole God's ark. It was the same day they captured me and threw me into this dungeon."

Eben tried to imagine twenty years.

"Now," Taavi said, "here's where the mice come into the story. The Philistines stored the ark in a dark corner because it caused great damage to their idol god, Dagon. Soon mice filled up the ark. But one day the mice came out and they carried a plague with them. This plague spread to the people, causing them to die. Finally the Philistines connected the plague to the ark, and they sent it back to our people."

I Wonder . . .

I wonder why God caused the mice to spread a plague to the Philistines . . .

The Lost Ark

Eben shook his head. "But that can't be right. If the ark came back, why haven't I heard about it or why haven't I seen it?"

"I don't know," Taavi said. "When I met you yesterday, my first fear was that you didn't worship the Lord because the ark was lost. Now I'm afraid I must be right."

"We have to break out," Eben said. "We must search for the ark. If my family knew that God spoke, it would change everything. We would believe in God just like you do."

Eben thrust himself against the stone that had held Taavi in the dungeon for twenty years. The stone didn't budge. He pounded himself against the stone again. Tears came to his eyes, not because his shoulder hurt, but because his heart hurt.

Taavi hummed a low tune. Eben grabbed Taavi's hand. "Please, please. You haven't given up, have you?"

"God will work when hearts are ready," Taavi said. "We must be faithful. God will show us what to do."

Eben blew angry air through his lips.

"Sit," Taavi said. "And listen. I'll tell you the words from the stone tablets."

Eben caught his breath. He sat at Taavi's feet. Yes, he wanted to hear the words that God had spoken.

"This is what God wants you to know," Taavi said. "The Lord wants to be your God. 'I the LORD your God, am a jealous God. . . . I punish . . . those who hate me. But for all time to come I show love to all those who love me and keep my commandments'" (Ex. 20:5-6).

I Wonder . . .
I wonder what God's words of long ago mean for you today . . .

"When you look to me with all your heart, you will find me."

Jeremiah 11:13

For Taavi

Taavi broke into a spell of coughing. All that talking seemed to tire Taavi, and he fell asleep resting against Eben's shoulder. Eben stretched his outer robe over Taavi's curled-up body.

But the sound of stone crunched against the entrance to the dungeon. Taavi gripped Eben's arm. "The only time the stone moved twice in a day was when you came. Pray."

Eben searched for words like Taavi's. "Lord God, show us your way."

"Psst, Eben. It's me, Hapu. How are you doing?"

Eben pressed his face up to the crack. "I'm alive," he answered.

"My father got drunk last night," Hapu said. "He walked off the upstairs balcony. It killed him. Now I'm in charge of Ashdod. But I don't like my father's servants. Come and be my servant."

Hapu's plea reminded Eben of Jud. Jud always liked to be the boss, telling him to do this and that. He hated it.

"You'll have plenty of food and a fire," Hapu said.

Taavi muffled a cough in the back corner.

Hapu's fingers reached through the crack. "Is there someone else with you?"

Eben's mind raced—food and water for Taavi. He prayed—this time from the heart. "I trust you, Lord."

He called to Hapu. "A prisoner named Taavi. You want him?"

"Why not?" Hapu said. "I have a lot of positions to fill."

I Wonder . . .
I wonder if Eben knew who was really in control of Ashdod . . .

"I will be found by you," announces the LORD. "And I will bring you back from where you were taken as prisoners."

Jeremiah 29:14

The Birth of Moses
Exodus 1:11-14, 22; 2:1-10

I magine that you are the son or daughter of a king. Wherever you go, a bodyguard goes with you. This bodyguard watches so you won't trip on the sidewalk, checks the tires on your bike, and stands guard outside your room even while you sleep.

Mothers are something like bodyguards as they watch over their babies. Moses' mother kept closer guard over her baby than any other mother. Keeping him quiet was the way to save him from Pharaoh.

Both a bodyguard and Moses' mother give you a picture of how closely God watches over you. If you are a child of the heavenly King, use these words from Psalm 121 to remind you of God's care.

Litany	
Lambs	**Kids**
The LORD won't let your foot slip.	
	He who watches over you won't get tired.
He who watches over Israel	
	won't get tired or go to sleep.

Song for the Week
"If You But Trust in God to Guide You," *Songs for LiFE* 210

Prayer for the Week
Lord, you know everything.
You have power over all.
You are so big you can care for everyone.
Yet you also care about just one—me.
Thank you. Amen.

Missing

Talori dropped a cucumber seed into Eben's bowl of lentil soup. The pale green seed floated. She skipped around the table. Soon Eben would come with the other workers. He'd see the seed and know he should meet her on the rooftop after supper. Planting secret messages was her way of playing the spy game with Eben.

The LORD watches over you.

Psalm 121:5

Tonight, though, it was more than just a game. She had found a feather that Eben would like. The others didn't understand that every feather Eben collected helped him believe that they could be free from the Philistines—as free as the birds. Neither did they understand why she wanted to be a spy. It was hard keeping the secret until after supper. But she didn't want the others to see the feather and make fun of Eben.

Izaak, Jud, and Shaul came into the courtyard, noisier than ever. They jostled and wrestled. The younger cousins came next.

"Jud," she called, "isn't Eben with you?"

"I told him not to go down to the road, but he must have gone anyway. There was a Philistine chariot down there. I guess he was too curious to obey the rules."

Talori narrowed her eyes at Jud. She was sure it was a lie. "Then why didn't you go after him?" She pounced on Jud, digging her fingernails into his skin. Jerusha, Talori's adopted grandmother, locked her arms around Talori, lifting her off of Jud. Talori's body went limp against Jerusha's firm but loving hold. But inside, the anger stayed. Jud hadn't cared enough to watch out for his brother. Or, worse yet, Jud had let something happen to Eben on purpose.

I Wonder . . .
I wonder if you can think of any times when you could feel that God was watching out for you . . .

The Search Party

After Talori escaped from Jerusha's arms, she ran to the rooftop.

The evening fires across Mizpah no longer burned brightly. Gray smoke trailed across the sky. Eben would say the smoke rose up to the invisible God. Wondering about God made Eben different from the others.

Loud voices rose from the courtyard. Jud was arguing with his father about Eben. Aunt Lily was crying above the voices. Then it was silent.

Talori peered over the edge, looking down into the courtyard. Jud, Izaak, and Shaul tossed a stone back and forth. Jud's father appeared from a side sleeping room. He gave the boys bows and arrows. "Are you sure you don't need me?" he asked.

Izaak flexed his bow. "Uncle Jedidiah, you must stay here and comfort Aunt Lily."

"That's right, Father," Jud said. "Eben probably just lost his way. We'll find him."

"Wait." Talori ran down the stone steps. "If anyone is going, let it be me."

Jud spit. "You are the last person we'd take. There's too much fire in you."

"Especially in your hair," Izaak said, poking an arrow tip into one of her wild curls.

Jerusha smoothed Talori's hair. "My dear, let the boys take care of it."

Jud set a torch on fire. Then he led Izaak and Shaul outside.

Talori's anger turned into short hiccuping sobs. Three days ago Eben had been trapped in a cave. Jud and Izaak said that the boulder must have fallen in front of the entrance. Talori suspected that Eben's trouble then had come from her cousins. Was that the case now too?

> The LORD will keep you from every kind of harm.
>
> *Psalm 121:7a*

I Wonder...
I wonder if you can remember a time when there was nothing you could do to help someone you loved—except pray...

A Spy

Talori crushed a charred piece of wood under her sandal. "Jerusha," she said, "please let me go. I must find Eben before they do. Finding someone is like spying. You just have to know the right places to look."

"Your father has given me instructions for your care," Jerusha said. "And he doesn't want you to spy."

A gust of wind sparked the fire. Talori's hair blew around her face. "Father doesn't know that I *can* spy."

Again Jerusha smoothed Talori's hair. "Sometimes I think your father goes on so many spying missions because he sees your mother in you. But because she is dead, he can't love her. And he is afraid to love you."

"I know that," Talori said. "Everyone always tells me she died because I was born." She broke away from Jerusha. "But once Father sees that I am a spy, the same as he is, he'll not be afraid of me. He'll love me. Besides, I have to rescue Eben."

She ran to the gate.

"Spies don't flare up and get angry," Jerusha said.

Talori stopped in the dark shadow of the gate. A few houses away, a baby cried. She paused. The baby's mother would soon quiet the baby. But who would comfort Eben? She ran into the dark night. Sparks from Jud's torch touched the night sky not far ahead. *Be like a spy,* she told herself as she crept toward the flickering light.

I Wonder . . .
I wonder if Talori is the kind of person you would like for a friend . . .

The LORD will watch over your life no matter where you go, both now and forever.

Psalm 121:8

Spy Work

The torchlight up ahead did not move. Did that mean they had found Eben?

Talori lifted her tunic above her knees and ran. Just outside the blaze of the torch, she stopped. The fire flickered on the faces of Jud, Izaak, and Shaul. They played their stone-tossing game as if they didn't have a thing to worry about.

She dropped to the ground, edging closer.

Izaak spoke. "What are we going to tell your father and mother?"

Jud drew a dagger-shaped object out of his tunic. The blade was covered with a leather sheath. "We'll show them the knife jacket. Tell them that it was on the ground next to large Philistine sandal prints."

Izaak hopped around a rock as if he were a fighter. "So they'll think a Philistine left the leather cover behind because he kept his knife on Eben the whole time."

"Right," Jud said. "They'll never guess we sold Eben for a knife."

Shaul bowed in front of Jud. "You are as great as a god."

Jud stood, his feet spread apart and his shoulders back. "The Philistine gods demand that warriors not be afraid to hurt anyone. I've proven that, haven't I?"

Burning anger filled Talori. But before she moved, Jerusha's words came to her. "Spies don't flare up and get angry." She pounded the ground. A stone cut her knuckles. As she pressed the sore hand into the other, she noticed the stars above poking through the sky. Was Eben right? Was there someone beyond the stars who could help?

I Wonder . . .

I wonder how you can tell that Jud, Izaak, and Shaul don't know the true God . . .

> I look up and pray to you. Your throne is in heaven.
>
> *Psalm 123:1*

The Braggers

Talori ran back to Mizpah. At the gate, she looked up. The stars formed the same patterns as every other night. They had to have a master.

"Be my master too," she whispered. Could she believe there was a master, a Lord who would help her? Could she trust the Lord to keep her from becoming angry? If she stayed calm, the boys might tell her more.

The bowls of lentil soup were cold. She started a new fire and poured the beans and broth back into the cooking pot. As the soup began to bubble, Jud, Izaak, and Shaul stomped into the courtyard.

"You're back. You must be hungry." She filled their bowls. "No Eben?"

Jud looked at Izaak. Then he said, "No, but we found a knife cover. See the design in the leather—it's Philistine."

Talori pointed at the slim leather pocket. "You're smart finding a clue like this."

Jud turned the sheath over, studying it. "My guess it that a leather craftsman made it for the son of a lord."

"You know a lot," Talori said. "Too bad you don't know which lord."

Jud tossed his head back showing off his thick neck. "It would have to be Ashdod. The picture of the god, Dagon, from Ashdod is carved into the leather."

While the boys ate, Talori went to the storage room. She dug through battle clothes until she found a leather helmet that fit her. Tonight she would leave for Ashdod.

I Wonder...
I wonder if you have ever asked God to be your master . . .

We depend on the LORD our God.
We wait for him to show us his favor.

Psalm 123:2b

The Burning Bush
Exodus 2:11-4:17

Have you ever wanted to fix what was wrong between two groups of your friends? It's not easy. You can end up not being liked by either side.

Moses wanted to help his people. But he ended up just causing more trouble. So he ran away.

But God had another plan for Moses. God wanted Moses to go back to Egypt and free his people. To get Moses' attention, God spoke to him from a burning bush. The bush reminded Moses that the Lord who called him was a powerful God.

The God who made the bush burn may call you too. The God who created the sea, the sky, the stars, the snow and the rain, the wind and the flame may want you to help those who are crying or needy. With God's help you may be able to fix what is wrong between your friends.

Use God's words to Moses from Exodus 4:11-12 to remind you that when God calls, you are not on your own.

Litany	
Lambs	**Kids**
"Who makes a man able to talk?"	
	"It is I, the LORD."
"Who makes him able to see?"	
	"It is I, the LORD."
"Now go."	
	"The LORD will help you."

Song for the Week
"Here I Am, Lord," *Songs for LiFE* 243

Prayer for the Week
Lord, the cries and hurts of my friends
call out to me.
Let me hear your call in their pain.
Go with me.
Make me wise with words and gifts. Amen.

The Firelight

The directions the LORD gives are true. All of them are completely right.

Psalm 19:9b

In the courtyard Talori listened for night sounds. An owl hooted from the clump of sycamore trees. What would it be like to leave Mizpah and go farther into the dark night? If she did, could she find her way to Ashdod?

She removed the leather helmet. It was useless going up against Jud, Izaak, and Shaul. She slumped against the gate. Then she stumbled backwards as the gate swung open. Uncle Jedidiah had forgotten to latch it.

Was it a sign that she should go? The stars glowed with a fierceness that appeared impossible to dim. Yet how would her feet know where to go?

Her attention was caught by flickering firelight in the shallow valley between Mizpah and the steep hills. Step by step, she approached the light.

To the left of the fire, she found a boulder to hide behind. The tall shadow of a man moved next to the small blaze. A shiver raised the hair on her arms. What if it was a Philistine spying on Mizpah? But there wasn't a chariot or a horse.

If it was a spy, could it be her father? Feeling brave because of that thought, she moved closer, ducking from one rock to another. When she was several arrow lengths away, the man turned. The soft curve of the cheek and the straight nose that flared out at the nostrils told her that her guess was right. If only Father would open his arms and she could run into them. She sniffed. Why did her nose always run at times like this?

An animal-skin boot appeared beside her. "Talori!"

I Wonder . . .
I wonder if you ever wish you could have lived in the days of God's people in Israel . . .
I wonder if it would help you feel closer to (or farther from) God . . .

A Father's Daughter

Talori lifted her head to see her father's face. The lines around his face were not tight. She spotted his dimple. "You're not angry then," she said, "that I spied on you?"

"So that's what you are doing," he said. "You surprised me. Come over by the fire and let me look at you. You are so tall. How long has it been?"

"Two seasons, Father. Why didn't you come home?"

Father bowed his head. "It's hard to explain, Talori."

"Grandmother Jerusha says you can't love me because of my red hair—because it is the same as Mother's."

Father sighed. "Your mother's red hair was striking and different than the others in our family. But her heart belonged to the one true God. That counts more than what a person looks like on the outside."

He stirred the fire with a stick. Small sparks flew into the air. "I was thinking about you tonight," he said. "I made a promise to your mother that I haven't kept."

Talori held her breath. For the first time ever her father was talking about her mother. Did that mean he was ready to be her father?

"I never raised you to know the Lord," Father said. Tears ran down into his beard. "I left it up to Jerusha. Dear Jerusha was so kind to give a home to my brothers and sisters when the Philistines destroyed our home. But like my bothers and sisters, she carries the hatred against the Philistines. They all depend on weapons—they are afraid to trust the Lord."

The Lord. Talori leaned back, looking up into the black-as-soot sky where the lights sparked. "Then it is true," she sat up straight. "The Lord is true."

I Wonder . . .

I wonder if you know how important it is to tell people about God . . .

The law of the LORD is perfect. It gives us new strength.

Psalm 19:7a

Obey Your Father

The laws of the LORD can be trusted. They make childish people wise.

Psalm 19:7b

Talori wished that this time under the stars by the fire would last forever.

Maybe her father thought the same thing, because he added another fat log to the fire. "Father," she said softly, "can you take me to Ashdod? Eben is there. The Philistines have him."

Father blew a low whistle. "Are you sure?"

"There was a chariot here before sundown. Jud claimed it came from Ashdod. And after that Eben disappeared."

Father got off the rock and walked back and forth beside the fire. "I followed the track of that chariot," he said. "That's why I am camped out here tonight. I suspected some mischief. But to steal Eben doesn't make sense."

"There's more to it," Talori said. And she told about Jud's talk of trading Eben for a knife.

"Go back to Jerusha," Father said. "I'm going after Eben."

Talori reached for his hand. "Take me. Your firelight tonight called to me. It was a sign. And now that you've told me the Lord is true, I know I'm supposed to go."

"There's more to knowing the Lord than just following a light. God's law tells you to obey your father. And I want you safe with Jerusha."

Talori stood on a rock to face him. "How can I be safe where Jud is living? And how can I obey my father when he is gone?"

I Wonder . . .
I wonder if a child can understand God's law as well as an adult can . . .

A Choice

Talori's father scooped up a handful of sandy soil and tossed it on the fire. The smoke from the fire drifted up into the air. Without the fire, Talori shivered in the cool night air. But only the fearful shiver of waiting for Father's answer bothered her.

"You're coming with me," Father said. "Run up the hill to the house and leave a message with Jerusha while I roll up my tent." He removed the limbs that supported his tent made of rough camel skins.

With a happy heart, Talori leaped over the rocks in the valley and ran home. The leather helmet lay just inside the gate. She put it on her head. Then, picking up a broken piece of pottery and a metal stick, she scratched a tall figure next to a short one with wild strands of hair. She put the picture on the oven where Jerusha would bake the morning bread.

Jud snored as he lay sleeping on a mat in the courtyard. His outer wool garment was at the foot of his mat. She took it. Underneath the cloak was the knife in its leather case. Her thoughts rushed over the choices. The way Jud got the knife was worse than her taking it from him. Having a knife could be useful for her own protection. Besides, it might work to trade the knife back for Eben. Without hesitating any longer, she shoved the knife under her belt.

She finished getting ready by putting on Jud's leather cloak over her tunic. It covered the knife in her belt. Next she stepped into his thick badger-skin boots.

I Wonder . . .
I wonder if Talori did the right thing in taking Jud's knife . . .

Keep me also from the sins I want to commit. May they not be my master.

Psalm 19:13

A Knife or the Lord

The commands of the LORD shine brightly. They give light to our minds.

Psalm 19:8b

As Talori ran from the walls of Mizpah, she scanned the valley. Without the fire, the valley became one super-sized sleeping giant. She'd never find Father. Was it his plan all along to leave while she was out of his sight?

"Psst. Is that you, Talori? With a leather helmet?"

"Yes, Father," she said. "I guess you couldn't tell it was your fiery redhead."

Father smiled even though his face appeared tight and worried. "We need to move through many hills tonight. Can you keep up with me?"

She nodded and fell in place behind Father. At times her legs and sides ached so much she wanted to drop to the side and rest. The long cloak and big boots slowed her down. But if she stopped to take them off, Father would get too far ahead. Besides, the cloak covered up the knife.

All night they crossed the dark Ephraim hills. Then the stars faded from the sky. The hills blushed with color around Talori. She felt the warmth of the sun on her back. She turned around. The rising sun painted every hill that they had crossed during the night. The brilliance amazed her. "It's you again, Lord," she whispered. "You are the master of the stars and the sun."

The knife weighed heavy from her belt. She opened her cloak to look at it. The handle was carved with an image of the Philistine god Dagon. Her mind wrestled. Was it the Lord she trusted to rescue Eben or was it the knife?

I Wonder . . .
I wonder if Talori can put her complete trust in God . . .
I wonder if you can . . .

The Ten Plagues

Exodus 7-11

Have your parents or a teacher ever said to you, "If you do that, you will be punished"? If you are wise, you listen to their warning. You obey their rules.

Pharaoh ignored Moses' warnings. He continued in his mean and stubborn ways. So God kept sending more punishments.

Psalm 119:9, 14, 16 will help you remember that obeying God's laws brings true joy.

Litany	
Lambs	**Kids**
How can young people keep their lives pure?	
	By living in keeping with God's Word.
Following God's covenant laws gives joy,	
	just as great riches give joy to others.
Take delight in God's orders.	
	Don't fail to obey God's Word.

Song for the Week
"I Will Put My Law," *Songs for LiFE* 39

Prayer for the Week
Lord, your laws are fair.
Your laws keep me safe.
They make me grow
straight and beautiful
like a tall shade tree.
Thank you for all of your words. Amen.

Trust

Talori had kept close to Father during the night. But now that there was more light, she allowed him to get further ahead. Then she yanked the knife from her belt. Should she get rid of it or not? Her fingers touched the sharp edges. It was a fearsome knife. And the fish-man carved into the handle frightened her like a monster in a dream.

"Talori."

Her head jerked up to see Father coming back toward her. Quickly she dropped the knife and stood in front of it.

"You did well keeping up with me through the night," Father said. "But we can't rest until we get to Gibeon." He swooped her into his arms.

There wasn't time to grab the knife. Would he be angry to know she had a Philistine knife? She breathed easier when it was obvious that he didn't see it.

With Talori riding on Father's broad shoulders, they angled down the hill into Gibeon. At the bottom, Talori turned and looked back into the hills. She told herself that under Father's strong care she didn't need the knife.

Father lowered her to the ground. She followed him through the winding streets of Gibeon to a stone house. A small man with flowing white hair met them at the door. "Zared, you're just in time. Are you ready to go to Kiriath-Jearim?"

Father introduced the man as Gili. Then Father and Gili talked about some kind of ark. They didn't mention Eben. Talori grew restless. When Father disappeared with Gili around the back of the house, she left and headed back up the hill for the knife.

I Wonder . . .
I wonder why Talori changed her mind about the knife . . .
I wonder if she changed her mind about God . . .

May the LORD answer you when you are in trouble.

Psalm 20:1

On Her Own

Talori climbed the hill to the spot where she figured the knife would be. After circling the area she found it. She shoved the gruesome-looking thing under her belt. But it didn't give her the security she wished for. She pushed away the thoughts of trusting the Lord and Father. After all, didn't Father trick her, making plans with Gili?

Or was it her mind that tricked her? Wasn't she afraid last night for nothing, thinking that Father had left without her? She hurried down the hill.

When she reached the streets of Gibeon, Talori didn't know how to find Gili's house. All the streets looked the same—narrow and winding. What if she never found Father? The way back to Mizpah through the Ephraim hills was a dark maze in her mind. And she didn't have the slightest idea which direction to turn for Ashdod.

Talori sat in the street and cried. What was wrong with her? Why did she get angry so quickly? But worst of all, her lack of trust in Father had ruined any hope of rescuing Eben. She was alone, hungry, and lost. She cried harder than she had all the times Jerusha punished her for getting angry and breaking a jar or a bowl.

The long legs of a horse stopped beside her. "Why did you leave?" It was Father's voice. "I've been looking all over for you."

Talori stood. With the blade lying across both of her uplifted palms, she offered the knife to Father. And as she told him the story, his face grew sad and still.

I Wonder . . .
I wonder why Talori's story made her father look sad . . .

Some trust in chariots. Some trust in horses. They are brought to their knees and fall down.

Psalm 20:7a, 8a

Another Chance

May he give you what your heart longs for.

Psalm 20:4

Father got off the horse. He supported Talori's foot for her to climb on the horse. Then he tossed the knife into the bushes and joined her on the horse. "There is so much I need to tell you," he said. "And so much about the Lord that you have never learned."

As Father guided the horse away from Gibeon, Talori leaned against his rough camel-skin tunic. His voice was low and sweet against her ear. "Gili has gone ahead of us."

"Will he help rescue Eben?"

The horse broke into a sweat before Father answered. "Gili went to Kiriath-Jearim. It's been our plan for several weeks. We heard the ark of the Lord is there. We're going to find out."

"But Father, I trusted you. I gave you the knife. How could you forget Eben?"

"Eben is still in the plan," Father said. "But the ark is holy. When I was a boy, the ark let us know God was with us. If we stop in Kiriath-Jearim, we can bring news of the ark to Eben. Kiriath-Jearim is on the way to Ashdod."

Dark storm clouds raced over the blue sky. Father urged the horse to go faster up a steep hill. A new eagerness to know more about this ark and the Lord excited Talori. And it touched her with a closeness to Father and Eben.

I Wonder...
I wonder if you feel eager to learn more about God . . .

The Secret on the Hill

When Talori and Father rode into Kiriath-Jearim, Gili met them at the main corner.

"We're wasting time," Gili said. "When I mentioned the ark to the people, they stared at me as if I were crazy. There's nothing in this little village."

As Father talked to Gili, Talori watched a man dressed in a ragged robe with dust on his forehead. She noticed him studying a high mound just ahead.

"Then we don't have a choice," Father said. He turned the horse around.

"Wait, Father. There's something up there." Talori pointed. "See the white stones of a house in the cedar trees?" She explained how she followed the gaze of the man.

Neither Talori or Father said a word as Father guided the horse up a narrow rocky path. Gili followed. Before they reached the house, a man as brown as the earth came out to meet them. His shoulders were broad, and his arms and legs were like large tree limbs. Talori pressed her face against Father's coarse camel robe. What would this fearsome-looking man do?

"The road doesn't go through," he said. "Turn around now."

Father cleared his throat. "What do you know about the ark of the Lord?"

The man lifted his heavy eyebrows. "I'm Eleazar, the son of Abinadab. Haven't you heard of those who died from touching the ark? Everyone is curious. But the Lord knows the respect is gone from the hearts of the people. Again I tell you. Leave!"

I Wonder ...
I wonder why it's important for us to show respect for God ...

The LORD knows what people think. He knows that their thoughts don't amount to anything.

Psalm 94:11

The Ark Is Returned

Talori pressed her legs against the horse's sides. It kept her legs from trembling.

"It's your job to keep us away," Father said, "so we'll leave now."

"No," shouted Talori. "All the way up here I've been thinking—if it's the Lord calling me to find Eben, then I want to know the Lord. I want to hear God's words."

Eleazar's heavy eyebrows came close together. "What the girl says is pleasing—it is what the Lord wants to hear from the people."

Talori, Father, and Gili got off their horses. They sat on a white stone.

With his great voice and great arms, Eleazar began the story. "The Philistines captured the ark, but wherever the ark went, the people became sick with a plague. They had heard that God sent plagues to the Egyptians when they were stubborn against the Lord. So they loaded the ark of God on a new cart. They hooked the cart to two cows who had new calves. Then they locked the calves away from their mothers. They wanted to see if the cows would return to their calves or take the ark back to the Israelites. Since the cows went straight to an Israelite town, the Philistines knew it was the Lord who brought the plague and was with the ark" (1 Sam. 6-7:1).

"Is God punishing us now because we are stubborn?" Talori asked.

Eleazar sighed. "Twenty years ago, when the ark came back, the people were like they are now. They do not follow God's command to put God first. Their hearts belong to themselves. So God allows the Philistines to run through our land and our cities."

I Wonder . . .

I wonder what "their hearts belong to themselves" means . . .

The LORD . . . wants to know whether you love him with all your heart and with all your soul.

Deuteronomy 13:3b

The Exodus

Exodus 12-14

One day in the middle of winter a mother told her son to pack a swimsuit, shorts, and T-shirts into his suitcase. She said they were going on a trip to a warm place. But the boy looked outside and saw snow. So he packed his boots and mittens.

After the mother showed her son pictures of the beaches and palm trees, he repacked.

When Moses first talked about leaving Egypt, the Israelites didn't have enough trust in God to leave. But God gave them ten pictures through the plagues. These plagues showed the Israelites that the Lord was God—the God they should follow.

This week use the words from Psalm 136:1, 11-13 to give yourself a picture of God.

Litany	
Lambs	**Kids**
Give thanks to the LORD.	
	His faithful love continues forever.
He brought the people of Israel out of Egypt.	
	His faithful love continues forever.
He did it by reaching out his mighty hand and powerful arm.	
	His faithful love continues forever.
Give thanks to the One who parted the Red Sea.	
	His faithful love continues forever.

Song for the Week
"Love Is Never Ending," *Songs for LiFE* 204

Prayer for the Week
Lord, you lead by your love.
You lead with power.
You lead to freedom.
Teach me to see that is who you are.
For your love is never-ending. Amen.

Thunder, Trust, and Glory

The LORD gives me strength. I sing about him.

Exodus 15:2a

Rain spit from dark clouds. Thunder rumbled boldly on the high hill of Kiriath-Jearim. Lightning pounced a stone's throw away from Talori, Father, Gili, and Eleazar.

"Are we going to die because we came to see the ark?" Talori asked.

Eleazar raised his brown arms upward. "Protect those who love you, Lord," he prayed. Then he ushered them into his cave. "Did you not come to hear the Lord's words?"

Talori thought about the tablets of stone. "Yes, God's words in the ark."

Eleazar crossed his arms over his broad chest. "God can't be held in a box. Has God given you strength to come up here?"

She nodded.

"Then you've met the Lord. Trust what God has already given you. And when all the people trust the Lord, God again will be with us in ways as magnificent and glorious as the golden ark."

Gili stood. "The prophet Samuel lives in Ramah. He is the one who can lead us back to the Lord. Zared, let's go to Samuel now."

A "no" shouted inside of Talori's head like the thunder outside. But why would Father want to rescue one little Eben when all of Israel needed to hear the message?

"Gili," Father said, "I'll catch up with you later. Talori and I are going to Ashdod to find Eben."

Then the horse carried Talori and Father down the hill.

I Wonder . . .
I wonder if you can think of something that reminds Christians today, like the ark reminded the Israelites, what a wonderful God we have . . .

Pomegranates and a Redhead

All through the night Father and Talori sped across flat land. Before sunrise, they stopped at a clump of palm trees. Father handed Talori a bundle. "These are merchants' clothes. Put them on."

Then he rubbed down the horse and tied it to a tree. "Entering Ashdod on a horse would draw too much attention to us."

Talori understood. Even so, her bottom lip trembled when they left the horse.

As they walked toward Ashdod, a beat thumped in her ears. Was a great Philistine army coming toward them? She caught Father's hand in her own. "What is it?"

Father squeezed back. "It's nothing to be afraid of Talori. It's the sea pounding against the shore. It's a very peaceful sound after you get used to it. Remember that the Lord created the sea. The Lord who we've asked to go with us."

As the early morning light gave way into bright blue sky, they followed other merchants through the front gates of Ashdod. The smoothness of objects amazed Talori—black and white squares painted on sleek jars and statues made glassy by iron tools.

"I'll spy around," Father said. "Stay in the market area. There are enough merchants that you shouldn't be noticed. But keep your ears and eyes open for any clues."

A bright spot of pomegranates attracted Talori. She stood next to the red fruit. "Lord," she whispered, "save us. I trust you—the one who has made all red things—even girls with showy red hair."

I Wonder . . .
I wonder what things you saw or listened to today that reminded you of God . . .

The LORD . . . has saved me.

Exodus 15:2b

The Procession

As Talori watched from behind the pomegranate basket, a loud commotion arose down the street. "What is it?" she asked the fruit seller.

The woman rushed into the street. When she returned, she pushed her baskets back to make more room. "It's Lord Hapu, coming this way. He has been chosen over his older brother to be the new lord of Ashdod. His father walked off a balcony, you know—dead as a rock now."

Talori nodded as if she knew all about it.

"Look at Hapu. Here he is now."

Talori leaned forward. Before she could stop herself, she screamed. Chained to the boy lord was Eben. Her screams went unnoticed, however, since everyone else shouted and screamed as well. Eben carried what looked like a person with skin so thin you could see right through to blue veins and bones.

Fighting back her screams, Talori ran to keep up with the procession, ducking in and out of the roaring crowd.

Just before the boy lord and the rest of his party reached the palace, Talori stood where Eben could see her. His mouth dropped open. Then Lord Hapu pushed Eben forward into the palace. The heavy doors closed.

After the crowd left, Talori hid behind a smooth white pillar. There was no doubt in her mind that Eben was shown to her on purpose. But how would she get to him?

I Wonder . . .
I wonder how you can tell God is taking care of Eben and Talori . . .

Because your love
is faithful, you
will lead the
people you
have set free.

Exodus 15:13a

A Piece of the Puzzle

"Psst, Talori." It was Father. "It was easy to spot your red head running through the crowd. That was very dangerous."

Before Talori could explain, a boy dressed in rich robes dropped a white feather beside their feet.

Father stooped to retrieve it for the boy. As he handed it to the boy, the boy said, "Taavi and Eben thank you." Then he backed away and reentered the palace.

Talori grabbed Father's hand. "That was Eben's feather. I'm positive Eben is sending us a message. I think he wants us to free him. His feather means freedom to him." Then she explained how she saw Eben chained to the boy lord. And about the bony body that Eben carried.

Father grabbed Talori's hand. "Come—I know a secret water tunnel that leads into the palace."

Behind the palace, they crawled through a thicket of bushes and entered a tunnel that descended underground. First they walked through the waist-deep water. Then they followed carved stone steps that led upward to a door in the palace floor. Here they rested.

"The name Taavi," Father said. "It has been haunting me. I once knew a Taavi from Bethel—he was about my age. He was stronger than anyone. He could plow a field in a day. The last I heard about him was from the battle with the Philistines at Shiloh. That was at least twenty years ago. Supposedly the Philistines brought him here to Ashdod. But I never guessed he could still be alive."

The sight of the bony man with a few white hairs like threads from an old cloth flashed back through Talori's mind. What if this was the strong boy, Taavi, that Father remembered?

"Talori, wait here," Father said. "I'm going up. Even if it costs my life I have to try and save them."

"I can't stay here," Talori said. "If anything happens to you, it'll have to happen to me too."

I Wonder . . .
I wonder if you know someone who has lived a long time and could tell you wonderful stories about God's care . . .

The LORD goes into battle. The LORD is his name.

Exodus 15:3

Chike

Father pushed against the door in the palace floor. After he disappeared through the opening, Talori followed. But Father didn't reach out his hand to help. When her head poked through the opening she knew why. Soldiers held Father's hands.

"Bring them to my quarters," ordered the boy who had earlier tossed the message.

When Talori and Father entered the room the boy dismissed the soldiers. "Are you Israelites?" he asked.

"Yes," Father said. "Who are you?"

"I'm Chike, the oldest son of the dead lord," the boy answered. "I was raised to be with my mother. I never received honors like my younger brother, Hapu. After Hapu was made lord, I begged my servant to explain this to me. He told me I'm an Israelite."

Talori stared at this boy's Philistine skirt and his iron sword. "How can it be?"

"My mother was forced to sacrifice her firstborn son to our god. It caused her to weep for days. So my father stole a baby from the Israelites."

Father jumped up and touched Chike's face. "Do you know where in Israel?"

"Mizpah," Chike answered.

Father's voice trembled. "Eben's brother was stolen too. You would be that age."

"Eben? The boy Hapu has chosen to be his servant?"

"Yes." Father spoke as if all the strength of thunder was in his bones.

"Then I will carry out my plan," Chike said. "I'll call for my chariot. We're leaving tonight. All of us—Eben, the man Taavi, and both of you."

I Wonder . . .

I wonder if your family has a story about a miracle God has done in your lives . . .

LORD . . . You do wonderful miracles.

Exodus 15:11e

Manna and Quail

Exodus 16

Who is the most thankful person you know? If you can't come up with an answer right now, spend some time this week looking for thankful people.

The Israelites should have been thankful. God had saved them and was leading them to their own land. But after six weeks in the desert, they sort of forgot to be thankful. After all, they were hungry. So they complained.

Perhaps you know God has saved you from your sins through Jesus. And you know there is a place in heaven for you. But when big and little things go wrong, you may forget all that God has done and has promised to do.

Use the words from Hebrews 12:28 and 13:5b to help you remember to be thankful this week.

Litany	
Lambs	**Kids**
We are receiving a kingdom,	
	a kingdom that can't be shaken.
So let us be thankful.	
	Be happy with what you have.
The LORD will never leave you.	
	The LORD will never desert you.

Song for the Week
"The Wise May Bring Their Learning," *Songs for LiFE* 70, stanza 3

Prayer for the Week
Lord, thank you for my friends, family, and fun times.
Thank you for the sky, sun, and Sundays.
Thank you for water, waffles, and the world.
But most of all thank you that you are God—
the God who loves, saves, and blesses. Amen.

Left Out

Once you were slaves of sin.

Romans 6:20a

Csilla's blue-black hair fell over her face as she bent over taking the bread out of the oven. Ouch! She burned herself on the hot stones. Not only did her hair smell of smoke, she had scorched her best tunic, and now there was a painful red burn on her hand.

"Jerusha," Csilla called to her step-grandmother. "Talori is back now. Make her do the baking."

"You did a good job while she was gone," Jerusha said. "I need you to help for just a few more days. Talori got very little sleep while she was away."

Csilla sat on a cold stone in the courtyard. The smoke of burning bread rose out of the oven. But she didn't care. If Talori was so tired, why wasn't she sleeping instead of being the center of attention with her stories?

Before Talori went on her adventure, it was Csilla's stories of the market that were the most exciting. All the colors, smells, and rich merchants enchanted the others.

Now it was Talori's story of finding Eben, Eben's story of being thrown in the dungeon with Taavi, and Taavi's story of God's plan in the whole situation. Finally it was the big story of how Chike was really her lost cousin, Chiram.

Csilla couldn't even count the number of times Talori told of how they all laid low in the bottom of Chiram's chariot. Then they rode out of Ashdod without a bit of trouble.

Jerusha hurried around feeding Talori, Eben, Chiram, and Taavi treats of dates and honey cakes from her cellar. And Csilla was expected to help with that too. It wasn't fair. Talori used to be her favorite cousin. But now Csilla hated her.

I Wonder . . .
I wonder if you know what it feels like to be jealous . . .

Two of the Same Mind

Csilla gathered together her baskets. The last four baskets she had made were not her best work. The weaving was uneven and loose. But she decided to take them to market anyway. It was better than staying around listening to Talori.

As Csilla opened the courtyard gate, no one noticed her leaving. Neither did they bid her success and good wishes for the day.

Outside the courtyard walls, Csilla stood and listened. Taavi's raspy voice spoke of the Lord. Little prickles crept over her skin just thinking about the strange skeleton man who was blinded by the sunlight. For twenty years he must not have thought of anything else besides the Lord because that was all he could talk about now. How could anyone know an invisible Lord? And especially anyone locked up in a dark dungeon?

"Csilla."

She jumped. It was Jud calling to her. That was a surprise. He usually ignored her or treated her like a child.

"Want some company?" he asked. "I have to get away from the house. Father isn't going to heat up the copper ovens today. He says there is too much to learn from Taavi. I smell a rat. How could Taavi live for twenty years on bread crumbs and water?"

Csilla eyes grew wide. Jud's doubts made her feel better.

Jud shifted a bundle that was under his arm. "That Chike or Chiram is a fake too. If he was really my brother, I'd know. He's a Philistine, and he's here to trap us."

I Wonder . . .

I wonder how you would answer Csilla's question: "How could anyone know an invisible Lord?" . . .

At that time right living did not control you.

Romans 6:20b

A Market Plan

Don't you know that when you give yourselves to obey someone, you become that person's slave?

Romans 6:16a

"What do you think about Talori's stories?" Csilla asked Jud.

"She had to come up with something. It's her excuse for stealing from me. You know she took my helmet and my cloak. And my new iron knife."

Csilla squirmed. She hadn't paid close attention, but hadn't Talori given back the helmet and coat? And didn't the knife belong to someone else? What should she believe?

Jud interrupted her thoughts. "The iron-wheeled chariot is down by the caves. I'm thinking of taking a little trip—you know, checking out their story."

"May I come?" Csilla asked.

Jud spit. "You're just a kid. But I was thinking. You often have silver pieces in your pouch. I could buy you something when I get to Ashdod."

Csilla touched the tip of her nose. Nose rings were popular with many girls at the market. Then she sighed. "I won't have any silver until I sell these baskets."

"I'll help you," Jud said, grabbing the baskets from her arms.

At the market, Jud hurried around showing off Csilla's baskets. It didn't take him long to sell all four. "See you," he said, leaving Csilla standing in the marketplace.

Jud was gone with the money. He had never really asked what she wanted. It was just a trick because he needed money. Now Csilla felt cheated out of a nose ring. After all that had happened, she deserved one— even if it wasn't from Ashdod. Nearby a crowd gathered around the stall where the woman sold gold jewelry. Csilla wriggled to the front.

I Wonder . . .

I wonder if you've ever been in a situation where one bad choice led to another . . .

—144—

Caught

Csilla picked up a tiny, gold nose hoop from the merchant's blanket. "That's a perfect one for you," said the woman seller. "You have the prettiest little nose, and the polished gold—ahh—it is so beautiful with your rich-colored skin. For you it's only twelve pieces of silver. Give the coins to my helper."

The woman left the ring in Csilla's hand. Then she stretched to help another buyer. Csilla closed her fingers over the gold band and stepped back into the crowd.

But her stomach didn't feel right. Maybe it was because she left home without bread this morning. If she had bread to eat, it'd be better. At the town baker's oven she glanced around. No one was looking. Quickly she snatched a loaf and ducked into the crowd. Leaving the market, she walked the side streets until she found a cranny in an old wall.

After she had taken two bites of the bread, Csilla heard scraping against the dirt. Someone small and dirty crawled toward her. The little dirty person with a torn tunic sat watching with wide eyes. "Go home," Csilla said. "Ask your mother for bread."

"Dead," the little creature said. "All dead."

Csilla thought about how Jerusha said bread was life. She tore off a piece. Stolen bread kept people alive too, didn't it? She handed it to the dirty child.

"Stolen?" The girl questioned Csilla with large eyes more than with her words. "They come and kill you when you steal."

I Wonder . . .
I wonder if you've ever had that bad feeling in your stomach that comes from doing something wrong . . .

You can be slaves of sin. Then you will die.

Romans 6:16b

Confession

There were stories around the market about people who were killed for stealing. Csilla guessed that was what had happened to the girl's family. Pains pinched her stomach. She tossed the bread. The birds who had been pecking in the dirt flew over to the scraps. "Stay here and watch the birds," she said to the girl.

Then Csilla ran back to the market. The woman selling the gold rings was still there. "I stole this," Csilla said. "Please, don't punish me."

"I believe you took it," said the woman, "but I can't believe you are returning it. I didn't catch you, so why?"

Csilla stumbled over some words. Then the answer came clearly to her. "Go to the house of Jerusha. There's a man there named Taavi. He knows all about the Lord and how to live."

She ran back to the girl. "Come home with me. I know how to make stew and bread." Csilla smiled at how good it felt to say that.

On the way home, the girl identified herself as Rinnah.

After Csilla fed Rinnah and bathed her, she put her to sleep on a clean deerskin. There was so much to learn about treating someone the right way. Her heart ached for the answers. The memory of Taavi's voice soothed something in her mind. It was his joyful thanksgiving and trust in God that drew the others to him.

I Wonder...
I wonder why helping Rinnah made Csilla feel good...
I wonder how you try to help others...

Now give your bodies to be slaves to right living. Then you will become holy.

Romans 6:19e

God's Law

Exodus 19-20

Think of something that is far, far away. Now think of something that is very close to you.

Could those two things be the same? They would be if you chose God. God in heaven is far away, yet God also can be in your heart.

When God gave the law to Moses, God's voice was like thunder on the mountain. God was so holy, the people could not even come close to the mountain. Everyone trembled with fear. Yet through Moses, the people were given words and thoughts from the mouth of God.

The words from Deuteronomy 30:11-12, 14, 16a will remind you how close God's message is to you.

Litany	
Lambs	**Kids**
What I am commanding you is not too hard.	
	It isn't beyond your reach.
It isn't up in heaven.	
	And it isn't beyond the ocean.
The message isn't far away at all.	
	It is really near you.
It is in your mouth	
	and in your heart.
You can obey it.	
	Love the LORD your God.

Song for the Week
"Love the Lord," *Songs for LiFE* 75

Prayer for the Week
Lord, your commands teach us to love—
to love you above all,
and our neighbor as ourselves.

You've given us that message.
May it always be on our hearts,
on our tongues, and in our
actions. Amen.

A Leader?

Early in the morning, before the first meal, Izaak hurried to the hunter's shed. He removed his eleven bows from their hooks. It had been his goal to build and use the strongest bow possible. And his example made him the leader of his cousins. But a bow didn't rescue Taavi from twenty years of captivity. It didn't make a home for the orphan girl, Rinnah. And it certainly didn't keep Jud from leaving home.

A tall shadow fell on the ground next to him. It was Chiram standing against the early morning sun. A white pigeon rested on his shoulder.

"That's an unusual pigeon," Izaak said.

Chiram coaxed the bird onto his hand. "This is White Vision. She followed me here. In Ashdod men trained pigeons to deliver messages during battle. But this one just circled the battlefields, never delivering messages. The Philistines believe that if you're not useful in battle, you're worthless. So the executioner was called to chop off its head. But I rescued it."

Izaak snapped the string of a bow. It stung against his bare arm. "Do you think it is different here?"

"When Taavi told me about the God of Israel, I got so excited. Right away I believed in God—the one who made us. But when we came here, I couldn't understand all the talk of hate and fear. Why doesn't having a living and loving God make any difference in the way people live?"

"It's because . . . "—Izaak thought about the fear that caused him to put everything into bow making—" . . . because we lost our way, thinking our strength was in our own power."

I Wonder . . .
I wonder what it means to "think our strength is in our own power" . . .

The LORD our God is near to us every time we pray to him. What other nation is great enough to have its gods that close to them?

Deuteronomy 4:7

Destroyed

Izaak thought about how they always bowed down to the idols, asking for more weapons, more grain, and more rain. It sounded so foolish after thinking about the true God, the one who made all things.

"Chiram," Izaak said. "We have to get rid of *all* the idols. Taavi said worshiping them goes against the true God."

The boys ran through the work sheds and through the house. They brought six sacks full of idols to the breakfast table.

"Father," Izaak said, holding up two sacks, "why do we have so many idols?"

Kilion, Izaak's muscular father, dropped his sharpening tool. "Life isn't easy. We've brought in gods to bless our pottery work, our hunting success, and our metal making. I never figured the Lord God could take care of it all."

"But we lost Jud because we put too much trust in things. Isn't Jud worth more than that?" Izaak said, bowing his head. "If only Jud could forget what I taught him and trust in God."

There was silence around the table. Then Kilion and his wife, Atalie, stood by their son, Izaak. "You acted the way we taught you. But now that we know the way of God, you are right: every idol must be destroyed."

Aunt Lily ran into the room behind the courtyard. When she returned, she carried a golden idol as if it were burning her hand. "Lord, forgive me for leading my son Jud astray."

I Wonder . . .
I wonder why it's hard to trust in God alone . . .

So be careful to do what the LORD your God has commanded you. Don't turn away from his commands to the right or the left.

Deuteronomy 5:32

— 149 —

Samuel

From the high hill of Mizpah, Izaak and his family threw the idols down the rocky slopes. The idols crashed into stones, smashing in hundreds of dusty pieces.

Uncle Zared came riding by on his horse. "I just came from the house," he said. "No one was there. And food was still on the table. What is happening?"

"Father," Talori said, "look what we've done. We've smashed all of our idols."

Uncle Zared raised both hands into the air. He laughed as if a deep spring bubbled up from the ground. "Your timing couldn't be better. I just came back from Samuel in Ramah, and he's meeting us tomorrow at the Mizpah well. All throughout Israel, Samuel is calling the people to return to the Lord."

***

In the morning, Izaak ran through the narrow streets. The crowd was so large, he couldn't see the well or Samuel, the man of God. He climbed a nearby courtyard wall so he could see over the crowd. Samuel spoke to the people. "Commit yourselves to the Lord. Serve God only. Then the Lord will save you from the powerful hand of the Philistines."

Samuel filled a pitcher with water from the well. He poured it out on the dry, rocky ground of Mizpah. In Mizpah, water was precious. No one wasted water on the places where the soil was hard and stony. So Izaak knew that pouring out the water was a way of saying they'd give up everything for the Lord.

Then Samuel prayed. And Izaak prayed too, asking God to forgive him. Next he prayed that Jud would hear God's call.

I Wonder . . .
I wonder what it means to give up everything for the Lord . . .

Keep all of his rules and commands I'm giving you. If you do, you will enjoy long life.

Deuteronomy 6:2b

Warnings

There was no eating or celebrating for the people that day. It was a day to humble themselves. They listened to Samuel's words from the Lord. "Turn away from false gods. Remember the Sabbath day. Do not steal. Do not murder. Do not want what others have." All the ways of God that the people had ignored and forgotten.

Izaak saw his father's tears fall to the ground. Strong Kilion, who wouldn't even cry if an arrow pierced him. Then, from Izaak's viewpoint on the wall, he saw a flash of metal. It was in the valley below Mizpah. If only it was Jud. Izaak had to know who was out there. As fast as his heart was racing, he ran the ring path to Mizpah's city gate and made his way to the lower valley.

"Jud!" He called out to the trees and rocks. "Please, let it be you."

On the third call, Jud jumped onto the trail with Izaak. A Philistine feathered helmet was on his head. And he carried a shield made of bronze and iron.

Izaak stood tall to face his cousin. "Come back to us. It's not too late."

"Think for yourself," Jud said. "The Israelites have turned into fools listening to Samuel. They have put away their swords. Don't you know better?"

Izaak could hear the sounds of marching boots in the distance. The clank of swords against armor grew louder as the bellow of war trumpets came closer.

"Mizpah, with its view of the valley, is a Philistine prize," Jud said. "And I'm leading the army the secret way up the back side."

I Wonder . . .
I wonder if you know someone like Jud, who thinks it's foolish to trust God . . .

The LORD is our God. The LORD is the one and only God. Love the LORD your God with all your heart and with all your soul. Love him with all your strength.

Deuteronomy 6:4-5

The Battle

Izaak feared the anger in his cousin's iron-black eyes. He ran back to Mizpah. His sides and chest hurt as he ran into the thick crowd of listening people. "The Philistines are coming," he called in between catching his breath.

The people called out to Samuel, "Don't stop crying to the Lord our God to help us. Keep praying that God will save us from the powerful hand of the Philistines."

Samuel called for a young lamb. Then he sacrificed it as a whole burnt offering to the Lord. He cried out to the Lord to help Israel (see 1 Sam. 7:7-9).

As the smoke from the offering rose upward to heaven, the Philistines barged into the streets of Mizpah. Their war cries were chilling. But louder than their wildest shouts crashed explosions of thunder. Suddenly the Philistines were running into each other. It was as if they didn't know which direction they should take.

"After them," cried Kilion.

The men of Israel chased the Philistines out of Mizpah. They didn't stop until the Philistines toppled off the cliff (1 Sam. 7:10-11).

Izaak walked home, his heart still pounding from the sight of the Philistines leaping to their deaths. Was it the end of Jud too? Izaak slumped beside the courtyard gate.

Taavi hobbled over and sat beside him. Izaak laid his head in Taavi's lap and cried.

I Wonder . . .
I wonder why it is so sad to see someone we love turn away from God . . .

The LORD our God commanded us to obey all of his rules. He commanded us to have respect for him. If we do, we will always succeed and be kept alive.

Deuteronomy 6:24

The Golden Calf

Exodus 32

In Deuteronomy 6:6-8 God said, "Write the commandments on your hands as a reminder. And tie them on your foreheads. Write them on the doorframes of your houses. And also write them on your gates."

God wanted the Israelites to always be close to their Lord. When their hearts weren't close to God, they were tempted by things around them—things like golden calves.

God knows a sinful heart keeps you from being close to your Lord too. So God did something very special. God sent Jesus from heaven. Talk with your family about how Jesus makes you close to God.

This week remember the words from Deuteronomy 6:4 and be close to your Lord.

Litany	
Lambs	**Kids**
The LORD is our God.	
	The LORD is the one and only God.
Love the LORD your God with all your heart and with all your soul.	
	Love him with all your strength.

Song for the Week
"Love God with All Your Soul and Strength," *Songs for LiFE* 76

Prayer for the Week
Lord, thank you for Jesus.
My heart goes my own way.
But Jesus gives me a new heart.
Now I can love you
with all of my heart, soul, and strength. Amen.

A Rebel

Dead Philistines lay scattered among the rocks on the sloping hillside. Jud crouched under a rock not far from the dead men. Evening shadows fell on him like preying lions. He shuddered. The thought of another hungry and cold night haunted him.

Last week it had made sense to join the brave, strong Philistines who had better weapons than the Israelites. He never expected the Philistines to lose all their wits and jump off the cliff at the sound of thunder. What took control of them?

Jud threw stones at the vultures that circled the dead bodies. He'd be their next victim if he didn't do something. If only things hadn't changed at home. It was all Eben's fault for searching for the creator God and then returning with that Chike who claimed to be their lost brother, Chiram. Now the talk at home was centered on trusting only one God. He kicked at the rock that shielded him. "I can't roll over, be weak, and say there is a God in heaven who controls all things."

More vultures swooped down. As they poked among the bodies, Jud thought about the iron-melting ovens these men had owned. Just knowing about their stashes of iron bars made him restless. Wasn't there something he could do?

He jumped up. Izaak could be his partner. Together they could operate the ovens and form their own weapons. Then Jud remembered Izaak's last conversation about God. Maybe he could trick Izaak by pretending to believe. Then he'd get Izaak to follow him. "Yes," he said. "I'll go back to Mizpah."

I Wonder...

I wonder why Jud thinks people who trust God are weak . . . and people who fight are strong . . .

LORD, you will give perfect peace to anyone who commits himself to be faithful to you. That's because he trusts in you.

Isaiah 26:3

The Celebration

Scrambling over rocks and thorny bushes, Jud climbed the last hill and returned to Mizpah. He crept past familiar stone houses. The evening fires in the courtyards burned low. Stealing through the darkness, he hurried to his home.

Slowly he opened the gate, keeping it from scraping against the stone wall. He let out a silent whistle of breath as he stood in the courtyard of his home. It was secure here—safe. Did he belong here after all?

Voices floated down from the upper room. The scent of roasted lamb lingered in the air. Jerusha only prepared lamb for celebrations. Were they rejoicing over the return of Eben and Chiram, or over defeating the Philistines? Well, whether they wanted to or not, they would celebrate that he was alive. Jud unfolded a deerskin blanket, spreading it out on the ground. Then he placed pottery, barley flour, honey, and all the leftover lamb into it. Before he tied the ends of the blanket, he listened to the chanting voices:

> *Who is God except the Lord?*
> *Who is the Rock except our God?*
> *He trains my hands to fight every battle.*
> *My arms can bend a bow of bronze.*
> *Your strong right hand keeps me going.*
> *You bend down to make me great (Ps. 18:31, 34, 35b).*

Who had a bronze bow? Was it a new weapon Chiram had brought back? Jud flexed his muscles. A rounded bump formed on his arm, but that wasn't enough to bend a bronze bow. He needed a plan to trap Izaak.

I Wonder . . .
I wonder why Jud can't understand what has changed . . .
I wonder if Jud's heart will change too . . .

Trust in the LORD forever. The LORD is the Rock. The LORD will keep us safe forever.

Isaiah 26:4

The Dugout and the Mole

The voices stopped their chanting. Then Jud heard the shuffling of feet. They were coming down the steps. He dropped his loot and escaped into the street.

Once he was in the street, he remembered how hungry he was. Why hadn't he taken a leg of roasted lamb? He wasn't being smart enough. But he wouldn't let it happen again.

For now he had to find a hiding place for the night. Not far from the tanner's shed was a dugout. It was a secret place that he and Izaak had made. They hid all their treasures in this place—broken Philistine arrows, pieces of pottery with secret messages, and colorful bird feathers. He congratulated himself for remembering the dugout and for finding it so quickly in the black night. Tomorrow he'd figure out what to do about food.

Inside the dugout, something smelled rotten. Tomorrow he'd clean it out.

He curled into a ball and closed his eyes. But his body trembled too much to sleep. What god would protect him and give him sleep? Golden statues of warlike gods and stone statues that demanded slashing of the body were the only ones that he could picture. His tired, aching body was wide awake.

A moving lump crawled over him, then another and another. Without thinking he screamed. The scream caused the creatures to scramble over him even faster than before. He caught one in his hand. It was a mole. A disgusting, hairy mole that couldn't even see.

I Wonder . . .
I wonder if Jud's family would take him back . . .
I wonder if God would . . .

Grace is shown to sinful people. But they still don't learn to do what is right.

Isaiah 26:10

Found

After killing several moles, Jud crawled out of the dugout. He went to the tanner's shed and buried himself under several tanned skins. In the morning the sun poured into the shed, but it didn't waken him. It was a brush of cool morning air that stirred him from his sleep. Izaak, who stood above him, had removed the skins.

"Jud!" Izaak shouted. "You're alive!"

Jud lifted up his head. Izaak's voice sounded cheerful and welcoming.

"I've been praying and hoping," Izaak said. "Since you knew about the cliff, it didn't make sense that you'd jump with the Philistines."

Jud spit, trying to get the dusty, hairy taste out of his mouth. "I came back for you," he said. "We can work together again—just you and me."

Izaak was quiet. Then he held his hand out to Jud. "Come, let's go home. Jerusha fixed a feast last night. There's plenty of lamb and lentils."

"Get it for me," Jud said, "and bring it back here. But don't let anyone know what you are doing. It has to be our secret."

Izaak straightened his shoulders. He stood tall and straight. His eyes looked steadily at Jud. Jud felt like a wild animal compared to his cousin.

"I will not steal for you," Izaak said.

Jud's thoughts spun around in his head like a chariot wheel that had broken and flown off the chariot. He wasn't fooling Izaak.

I Wonder . . .
I wonder who is guiding Jud . . .
I wonder who is guiding Izaak . . .
I wonder who guides you . . .

LORD, you are honest and fair. You guide those who do what is right.

Isaiah 26:7a

The Name of the Lord

The next thing Jud knew he was lying on his own sleeping mat in the house.

Izaak sat beside him. "Here," he said, holding out a bowl of broth. "Drink."

Jud took a sip. "What happened?"

"You blacked out," Izaak said. "Have you eaten anything the past few days?"

Jud heard concern in Izaak's voice, but his cousin had double-crossed him. If Izaak had brought the food in the first place, this would not have happened. Hot anger boiled inside of him. It was harder than he thought to act foolish over this God thing in order to fool Izaak.

"Remember you always said, 'Make your enemies afraid of you'?" he said to Izaak.

Izaak nodded. "Our enemies *are* afraid of us because of God. But we don't have to be afraid of our enemies. God's name is 'The One Who Always Sets Us Free.'"

"That's not a name." In his anger Jud clenched his teeth and twisted his fingers into a stiff curl. "A real name is one like Dagon or Baal."

"You can't fit God into one name," Izaak said. "The names of God are all the things our Lord does for us. That's how we know God."

"You fool," Jud said. "Your enemies will go after you like a wild bear after a lamb. You can't sit back and say the Lord will take care of you."

One of Jerusha's knives was nearby. He grabbed the knife and tossed it, just missing Izaak. Then he left. He ran out of the town gate and away from Mizpah.

I Wonder . . .
I wonder how many names for God you can think of . . .
I wonder if you know what each one means . . .

LORD, we are living the way your laws command us to live. We are waiting for you to act. Our hearts long for you to be true to your name.

Isaiah 26:8

Exploring the Promised Land
Numbers 13-14

Your promises may be as good as your memory—ever forget anything? Your promises may be as good as how you feel on a certain day—ever feel nasty? Or your promises may be as good as how much money you have—ever spend all your allowance on a movie or candy?

But God's promises to save people lasted through floods. Remember Noah? They lasted through old age. Remember Abraham? They survived through years of wandering in the wilderness. Remember Moses and the people? And if you know that Jesus came from God for you—you know that the promises have lasted for you. Are you waiting for God's next promise? There's a place in heaven for all believers, and that includes you!

Put your faith in God's promises with words from Psalm 138:1a, 2c, 8.

Litany	
Lambs	**Kids**
LORD, I will praise you with all my heart	
	because you are loving and faithful.
LORD, you will do everything you have planned for me.	
	LORD, your faithful love continues forever.
You have done so much for us.	
	Don't stop now.

Song for the Week
"We Are on Our Way," *Songs for LiFE* 100

Prayer for the Week
Lord, you are the God of promises.
You promised land for your people.
You promised salvation.
You promised love, joy, and peace through your Spirit.
You are my Lord and Savior. Amen.

Chiram and Taavi

Satisfy the needs
of those who are
crushed. Then my
blessing will light
up your darkness.

Isaiah 58:10b

Chiram pulled his new deerskin tunic over his head. The smell of the leather and the softness of the tunic against his body was better than all the fancy garments he had in Ashdod. Izaak had made it for him, and it fit perfectly.

"Thank you," he said. "I feel as if I'm home."

All of his cousins and his brother Eben circled around him as if they were the clay dishes and he was the stew pot. Everyone laughed when he described them that way. But Taavi's laughter turned into a coughing spell.

The cousins scattered to get things for Taavi—more blankets, a cup of water, and honey to soothe his cough.

"Would you like to rest on the rooftop?" Chiram asked. "The sun is stronger up there than down in the courtyard."

Taavi nodded, so Chiram gathered Taavi into his arms. Several of Taavi's brittle bones had broken, so none of the family let him walk anymore. All the older cousins could carry Taavi because he weighed so little.

As Chiram climbed each step, he wished there was something more he could do for Taavi. All of his years in Ashdod he had lived close to Taavi, but never knew it. Now his heart was so close to Taavi that it hurt thinking Taavi didn't have many days left. It wasn't fair. For all the dark and starving days that Taavi prayed and was faithful to God, wasn't there something special waiting for him?

I Wonder . . .
I wonder if Taavi thinks God has not been fair . . .

Dreaming of Bethel

As Chiram climbed each step with Taavi in his arms, Taavi whispered, "Thank you."

"Here we are," Chiram said when they stepped into the warm sunlight of the rooftop. "Where would you like to rest?"

Taavi pointed to the northwest corner. "Let me face Bethel. It is my boyhood home and perhaps still the home of my sister Sapphira."

Chiram lowered Taavi to the rooftop floor. As he fixed the mat and skins for a comfortable resting spot, a plan formed in his mind. Taavi wasn't strong enough to travel to Bethel. But why not find his family and bring them to Mizpah for a visit?

As Taavi's head bowed in prayer, Chiram shielded his hand over his eyes, looking over the land toward Bethel. Somewhere out there was his brother, Jud. And from the messages that Jud left at the gate, he was angry. But also out there was Taavi's sister and the possibility of giving Taavi a small gift of joy.

White Vision, Chiram's pigeon, came and sat on his shoulder. "What do you think, White Vision? Can we find Taavi's sister?"

White Vision cooed. Then she flew to the rooftop edge and flapped her wings.

"Taavi," he whispered, "I'm going to find Sapphira."

"Sapphira?" Taavi's voice quivered. "Is it possible?"

Chiram took a deep breath. Everything that was worthwhile took trust. It took trust to leave Ashdod. It took trust to believe in the LORD after all the years of living in luxury under the gods of the Philistines. "Yes, Taavi, it is possible."

I Wonder . . .

I wonder if you know someone like Taavi who could teach you more about trusting God . . .

> "I will always guide you. . . . I will make you stronger."
>
> *Isaiah 58:11*

The Meeting

I will march out
ahead of you.
And my glory will
follow behind you
and guard you.
That is because
I always do what
is right.

Isaiah 58:8b

Outside of Mizpah, Chiram watched for movement behind every rock and in every tree. His Philistine training taught him to always be aware of an enemy.

A flattened spot in the grass suddenly alerted all of his senses. With an arrow ready in his bow, he approached. Yes, there was a body lying in the grass. Was it dead or alive? "You on the ground," he called. "Do you need help?"

A moan rose from the grass. Kneeling on one knee, Chiram brushed aside the grass and faced his brother Jud. Jud's clothing was bloodstained.

Chiram lifted his brother's head and gave him a sip of water.

"You have to help me," Jud said. "Help me get home to Mizpah. Jerusha needs to take care of my wound. I told the Philistines that I wanted to worship the Lord in Mizpah. Then they shot me."

Chiram let Jud's head drop back to the ground. Could he believe this story after all of the nasty messages? Or was he falling into a trap? If he helped Jud, he might never find Taavi's sister in time. But he couldn't walk away from his very own brother.

Chiram stooped down to help Jud get up. It didn't take much. Even with the loss of blood, his brother seemed strong. White Vision's head bobbed back and forth as she walked nearby. Swiftly Jud reached for White Vision, catching her around the neck. "Don't think you can stare at me with those red eyes," he said.

Chiram saw Jud's strength. He had to think fast. "The army of the Lord," he cried. It worked. Jud let go to look. White Vision flew away and Chiram ran.

I Wonder . . .
I wonder what Chiram should do . . .

The Message

Chiram ran in the direction of Bethel. This time he didn't watch for enemies behind rocks or up in trees. He just ran.

Outside the stone walls of Bethel, he drank thirstily from the spring. Some children who were playing by the water ran when they saw him. Their frightened eyes reminded Chiram that even though he dressed like an Israelite, his hair still had the cut of a Philistine. And if he entered Bethel, he would cause fear and most likely be chased away.

"White Vision," Chiram said, "go into the town. Listen for the name Sapphira."

White Vision bobbed her head.

"Sapphira," Chiram repeated. "Get Sapphira to follow you back to me."

White Vision flew over the wall into Bethel. She was a smart bird, but this was the hardest task Chiram had ever given her. He tossed small pebbles into the stream, wondering what else he could do. The afternoon shadows were getting longer. Was White Vision in danger? Thinking of danger reminded him of Jud. Had Jud followed them, causing more trouble for White Vision?

He bowed his head. But his prayer was interrupted by a woman's loud, scolding words. She came out of the town gate, waving her arms and yelling, "Come back with my weaving thread."

In the sky above, White Vision was flying with a long thread trailing from her beak. Chiram laughed at the sight. Then, as the pigeon landed on his shoulder, he walked toward the woman, holding out her thread.

"You must be Sapphira," he said. "I'm Chiram from Mizpah. I've come with a message from your brother, Taavi."

I Wonder . . .
I wonder if finding Sapphira seemed like a miracle to Chiram . . .

You will call out to me for help. And I will answer you. You will cry out. And I will say, "Here I am."

Isaiah 58:9

Home

Chiram told Sapphira the entire story of Taavi.

Sapphira hugged and kissed Chiram. "I must tell Kyla, Jensine, Chuna, Martha, Yerick, Joel, Joosef . . ." she said, running back to Bethel.

Chiram waited. Then, like a great swarm of bees coming out of a hive, people followed Sapphira out of Bethel. They ran down the road. Chiram followed them. For six miles they ran, at times carrying the younger ones. When they came to Mizpah, Chiram led the way.

He brought the whole group to the rooftop. They surrounded Taavi, talking, crying, and hugging.

Then Taavi raised his hand.

"I must leave," he said. "I'm going to meet the great I Am. My Lord has been good to me. My God has allowed me to see you before I died."

Taavi closed his eyes. And his face seemed to glow as it became stone still.

Sapphira held on to her family and then Chiram.

"I thought he'd live if you came," Chiram sobbed.

"He is living," Sapphira said. "He went through the gates where God's glory shines forever. There he will live forever with God."

Sapphira and all those from Bethel stayed in Mizpah for a week. They remembered the words and ways of Taavi. They also bowed to the Lord in worship, promising to trust God for the rest of their days, just as Taavi had done.

And they prayed every day for Jud just as Taavi would have done.

I Wonder . . .
I wonder what was the most important thing Taavi did in all of his life . . .

You will not need the light of the sun by day anymore. The bright light of the moon will no longer have to shine on you. I will be your light forever. My glory will shine on you. I am the LORD your God.

Isaiah 60:19

Jerusalem

When David became king, he first built his palace in Hebron, a city in the land of Judah. Seven years later, when he realized he wanted to be closer to the people in the northern part of his kingdom, David decided to move his palace to Jerusalem. There was just one problem: Jerusalem belonged to the Jebusites. So before David could claim the city for his own, he had to conquer the people who lived there.

The people of God had often battled for this city in the past, but they were never successful. This time, with the help of commander in chief Joab, David was able to capture the city. Once David was settled and secure in Jerusalem, he wanted to bring God's ark of the covenant into the city. He hoped that once again the Israelites could be blessed with the presence of God. Through this and other commitments David showed that his desire was for God. And because of that Jerusalem became a great city.

When Jesus was on earth, his death and resurrection took place in Jerusalem. And it was in Jerusalem that the Holy Spirit came to the disciples.

In the book of Revelation we hear about the New Jerusalem—the city of God. This is the place where someday all of God's children will be present with their Lord.

Rooftop Kids of Jerusalem

Israelites

Abbie (11)

She is a loyal and faithful friend. She is proud that so many people come to her father for advice, and she wants to be wise like him. But what will she do when she thinks her understanding of a situation is better than her father's?

Jory (9)

He also respects and admires his father and hopes to be like him. But he thinks he can gain wisdom through an older friend. When he is confronted with making his own decision, he learns to depend upon God.

Carmeline (11)

Two years before this story began, Carmeline's family was sick with the plague. Her younger brother and sister died from it. Since God kept her alive, Carmeline thinks God is calling her to do something, but she isn't sure what that is. Meanwhile, she tries her best to obey her parents and God.

Ronia (11)

Ronia discovers riches can't give her all her desires. When she puts God first, she loses wealth but gains peace and joy.

Hezro (10)

He wants to explore his new surroundings in Jerusalem. He also likes to impress others with his knowledge of his discoveries. Jory is especially easy to impress.

Jehesah (11)

His father is a harp musician. Jehesah has been trained on the harp too, but he doesn't connect to the music—it never sounds just right. He must learn the secret of the harp.

Zarah (9)

She believes her music is something to give, so she plays in the streets, for friends, and for those who may be sad. Like her music, she is sweet, tender, and lyrical.

Elias (8)

He loves to make noise—any kind. He wishes he could play the large cymbals and make a clash of noise. But so far all he is allowed to play are the resounding cymbals—the small finger cymbals.

Jebusites
Matin (11)

He was born with the left side of his body weaker than the right side, so he has always needed a walking stick. His father was a Jebusite soldier who had a hard time being proud of his handicapped son. For a long time Matin hoped he could do something to please his father. But he discovers his hope is not in his earthly father.

Anoush (8)

She works hard as a water girl and tries to protect her brother, Matin, but she needs him more than she can watch out for him. She also needs the love of parents and God.

Jamila (11)

All the changes that have taken place in Jerusalem under the Israelites are puzzling to her. In some ways she wants to believe in God so she can be like the others, but the whole thing about God doesn't make sense to her. Her family decided to stay in Jerusalem if possible because they felt it was the best thing for her sister, Meryl.

Meryl (10)

She has been sick for a year. The doctors don't know what is wrong. She is getting worse instead of better.

Tarik (9)

He wants his family to stay in Jerusalem, not run away the way his Jebusite friends did. He hopes his father can work again as a stone cutter, and that he can work alongside his father. He worries about fitting in with the Israelites and whether their God will allow the family to stay.

Rahab and the Spies
Joshua 2

Would you like to be part of a team that won every game? It would be an exciting season, wouldn't it?

When the spies came to Rahab, she had already heard about the Israelite victories. She had heard about the God who parted the Red Sea for the people and drowned the enemy, Pharaoh. She could see that God had chosen to be with these people. So imagine how she felt when *she* was called to be a part of this team—the team of God's people.

We may never understand the mystery of how God chooses people, but we know that in the end God's "team" will be on the winning side. Echo the words of Ephesians 1:11, 14, and thank God for offering to put you on the greatest team ever.

Litany	
Lambs	**Kids**
God decided to choose us long ago	
	in keeping with his plan.
He works out everything	
	to fit his plan and purpose.
The Spirit marks us as God's own.	
	We can now be sure that someday we will receive all that God has promised.

Song for the Week
"Standing on the Lord's Side," *Songs for LiFE* 227

Prayer for the Week
Dear God,
Thank you for choosing me for your team.
I like standing on your side.
Fit me into your plans.
Put me in your game. Amen.

Soldiers!

Because he is proud, that evil person doesn't turn to [the LORD].

Psalm 10:4a

Matin stood high up on the Jerusalem wall with his father. It was a day of honor. The Jebusite king had assigned his father to be captain of all the soldiers who guarded Jerusalem's east wall. The first thing Father did was excuse two men from their duties. Matin watched the men slide silver pieces into Father's robe.

"Don't you need all of the guards?" Matin asked.

"It has been quiet for weeks," Father said. "The men must tend their fields outside the city. Besides, you're helping me. Even a disabled boy like you can see from one end of this valley to the other."

Matin shifted his weight on his crutch so he faced down the valley instead of toward Father. Couldn't Father be proud of a son with a lame leg?

He concentrated on the mountain across the valley. Something moved next to an olive tree. Could this be the day he would prove his worth to Father? His heart thumped. Then the mountainside darkened with the formation of soldiers.

"Father, look!" He pointed in the direction of the soldiers. "Is it an attack?"

Father shielded his eyes against the sun. Then he sent a warning out to all the guards.

"Are you afraid?" Matin asked.

His father puffed out his chest. "It's only King David and the Israelites. Those Israelites claim their God goes with them in battle. But they've never defeated Jerusalem. Our walls are greater than their God."

I Wonder . . .
I wonder if it is easier to trust things you can see rather than a God you can't see . . .

The Blind and Disabled

Matin listen as his father discussed a plan of action with the other guards.

"As they get closer," Father said, "we'll shout at them, insulting them until they feel small and puny. They won't even dare raise their arms against us."

More Jebusite soldiers and guards lined the walkway on top of the wall. With arrows aimed, they discussed insults.

Across the way, Matin spied the one who had to be King David. He had heard stories about this king. When David was a young boy, he stood up against a Philistine giant. Secretly David was Matin's hero. So often he had dreamed of talking to David, finding out his secrets. But now he had a chance to be a hero *against* David.

"Father," Matin said, looking into his father's face, "is it possible that the God of the Israelites can win any battle?"

Father spit. "It's bad enough that your body is disabled. Don't let your mind grow weak too. Can't you see we are a fortress high above the valleys? Walls like ours are mightier than any god. Just listen. I'll scare them away." He turned away from Matin and stepped close to the edge of the wall. He cupped his hands around his mouth and yelled. "You won't get in here. Even blind people and those who are disabled can keep you from coming in."*

The other Jebusites began chanting Father's words.

Matin punched his fist against his lame side. Who was Father making fun of, his son or the Israelites? But he couldn't feel sorry for himself. He had to do something.

I Wonder . . .
I wonder what *you* remember most about King David . . .
I wonder if you've ever wanted to be like him . . .

*2 Samuel 4: 6-8

There is no room for God in any of their thoughts.

Psalm 10:4b

The Gihon Spring

Sinful people say
to themselves,
"God doesn't pay
any attention. He
covers his face. He
never sees us."

Psalm 10:11

Matin squeezed himself into a small ledge formed by the peephole in the wall. Would the Israelites give up? Did the shouts that the blind and lame could defend Jerusalem actually impress them with the strength of the walls?

Off to the side of David's large group, Matin noticed a smaller group of David's men. They were creeping down the valley. He crawled out of the peephole and tugged on his father's armband. "A small army is coming this way."

"They heard our words," Father said. "If they come closer, they'll only see the great strength of our fortress."

Matin hobbled across the wide path of the wall away from Father. When he reached the tower, he paused, searching the valley for David's men. He didn't see them. Keeping in the shadow of the tower, he looked straight down along the wall. There they were, approaching the Gihon spring.

Did they have their sights on the tunnel that led from the spring and then went under the city wall? It was possible to travel through the rushing water in the tunnel. But the tunnel didn't lead directly into the city. A deep shaft separated the water from the city. When Matin and his sister Anoush had to get water from inside the city, they used a bucket on a rope—a rope eight times longer than a man. Should he remind Father of the shaft? No, Father would snarl, telling Matin that no man had ever climbed the tall slippery shaft and no man ever would. But Matin had to see for himself what David's men would do.

I Wonder . . .
I wonder why some people can only see their own strength and not the strength of God . . .

Inside the Tunnel

Matin hurried to the tunnel inside the city wall. It was dark inside except for a few small flickering lights. The women from the city had placed oil lamps along the path. Using the tunnel wall as a support and guide, Matin moved toward the shaft. A shadowy figure came toward him. He peered through the dimness. It was his sister, carrying a water jug!

"Anoush, what are you doing here?"

"Mother ordered water," she said. "The city gates are locked, so I couldn't go to the spring."

Matin put his fingers over her lips. "Shh. Listen," he whispered.

The sound of metal against stone echoed up the shaft and into the tunnel.

"What is it?" Anoush whispered.

Matin's fear controlled his heart and breath. He could hardly speak. "Armor clinking against the shaft walls. The Israelites are climbing up."

Anoush dropped her jug. Water puddled around their feet. "But you were with me when we dangled the lamp down into the shaft. You saw there were no places to grip your toes or fingers. A person would fall to his death for sure in that slippery cave."

The metal against stone clinks were getting closer. There was no time to escape.

"Hide, Anoush," Matin said, thinking he had said his last words. He pushed her down behind a jut in the tunnel wall. Then he squatted in front of her.

The soldiers appeared to be working as a team. Each soldier was pushed through the opening by one below. "The LORD will give us the city," said their leader.

I Wonder . . .

I wonder what made the soldiers say, "The Lord will give us the city" . . .

LORD, rise up!
God, show your power!

Psalm 10:12

New Worries

God, you see trouble and sadness. You take note of it. You do something about it.

Psalm 10:14

On the way out of the tunnel, one of the soldiers nearly brushed against Matin's leg. That leg just didn't bend enough to tuck behind the rock. The soldiers didn't see the children in the dim light, but for the third time that day, Matin hated his leg.

In his heavy-heartedness, he wasn't paying attention to the soldiers' words until he heard—"Blind and disabled people will never be welcomed in David's palace."

"What is the plan?" asked one of the others.

"We'll capture the guards at the east gate," said the leader. "Then we will let in David and the rest of the men. We'll fight those who go against us. Allow the others to run into the hills or remain in peace. But their idols must be destroyed."

All the men nodded.

"Let's go," the leader said. "God is our power."

Matin leaned against the boulder, allowing it to support him. These Israelite men had the city under their power, yet they said the power belonged to God.

Anoush pressed up against him. "What now?"

Matin wrapped his arm around her shaking body. Should they run and find their parents? But what if in the confusion they never found them? For sure their parents would escape into the hills when their gods were destroyed. And they wouldn't wait for a hobbling boy who slowed them down. "We'll stay here," he said, "until morning."

I Wonder . . .
I wonder what you would do if you were Matin and Anoush . . .
I wonder why God often reaches down to help those who are helpless . . .

Crossing the Jordan
Joshua 3-4

God told Moses. Moses told the people. God told Joshua. Joshua told the people. Jesus told the disciples. The apostle Paul tells it to all those who read his letters. What is it? It is the message that God is with you.

The Israelites experienced God's presence when they came to the Jordan River. They saw it was impossible to cross the deep river. But God was with them. God parted the water for a path. Then they followed the priests on dry ground between high water walls.

This week remember God's promise to you—I will be with you. And shout the words God spoke to Joshua in Deuteronomy 31:8.

Litany	
Lambs	**Kids**
The LORD himself will be with you.	
	He will never leave you.
The LORD himself will be with you.	
	So don't be afraid.
The LORD himself will be with you.	
	Don't lose hope.

Song for the Week
"Our Help," *Songs for LiFE* 219

Prayer for the Week
Lord, you are there when I am in school.
You are there on my way home.
You find me when I am scared.
You love me when I need forgiveness.
Don't let me forget that you are always with me. Amen.

The King Leaves

Abbie's best friend, Carmeline, was spending the afternoon on Abbie's rooftop in the city of Hebron. Using small stones, they outlined squares to make pretend houses.

"This is my house," Abbie said.

"And this is mine," Carmeline said. "We will always live next to each other."

Noises in the road below made the girls stop their play and watch a procession coming from the palace.

"It's King David," Carmeline said. "He's moving to the city of Jerusalem."

Abbie sat on the rooftop ledge with her friend. Once she had been in the courtyard of King David's palace, but she had never been inside. So it was wonderful to watch the movers carrying all the beautiful things that belonged to a king. "If I ever get a rug of many colors, I'll give it to you," she said to Carmeline.

"And if I ever get an ivory bed, I'll give it to you," Carmeline said.

The girls linked arms around each other.

While they watched for more kingly treasures, Jory, Abbie's younger brother, came up to the rooftop. He waved his arms and jumped around the girls. "Guess what," he said. "We're moving to Jerusalem. King David has asked Father to be a gatekeeper."

"Father?" Abbie clapped her hands.

"Yes," Jory said. "The king wants wise, brave, and honest men in his new city. And that means Father."

I Wonder . . .

I wonder if it you've ever wished you could go back in time and talk to God's children who lived in the days of King David . . .

I wonder what questions you'd ask them . . .

Your kingdom is built on what is right and fair.

Psalm 89:14a

Abbie's Disappointment

Abbie took hold of Carmeline's hands. "Jerusalem. Just imagine! Our dream might come true. I'll get a colored woven rug for you, and you'll get an ivory bed for me."

Carmeline broke away from Abbie. "My father won't leave Hebron. His fields are here. Our fields have been in his family since the tribe of Judah entered Canaan."

"But Jerusalem will be the city of the kings forever," Abbie said. "That's what my father said last night. Let's go tell your father." She reached for her friend's hands again, but Carmeline ran away and down the stone steps.

Abbie went after her friend, but before she reached the bottom of the steps, Father met her. "Did Jory tell you the news?"

"Yes, Father. Are more families moving? Because it'd be terrible if I had to leave Carmeline behind."

Father stroked his dark beard. "King David has not asked everyone. Some families will stay because of their fields. But Ronia's family is going. I believe Ronia is your age, so you won't be the only eleven-year-old girl."

Abbie clamped her teeth together. Father never allowed them to say bad things about others. She couldn't tell him that Ronia was always bragging and showing off new clothes and jewelry.

As the tears came to Abbie's eyes, Father wrapped his arm around her. "I know you've been best friends with Carmeline. Trust God to be with you *and* with your friend."

I Wonder . . .
I wonder if it will be easy for Abbie to follow Father's advice . . .
I wonder why it is hard to trust when things don't turn out the way you want them to . . .

Your truth and faithful love lead the way in front of you.

Psalm 89:14b

Gifts

In the morning, two of the king's donkeys arrived at Abbie's house in Hebron. Jory stirred through the saddlebags, shouting with excitement over the treasures sent by the king. Father excused Abbie from the packing to spend the last day with Carmeline. But instead, she went to the rooftop and dropped her stones off the side. She'd never play the pretend games with these stones again. If Father and Mother knew how angry she was, they'd say she was a thankless girl, so Abbie kept away from everyone.

The next morning, Mother said Abbie could ride a donkey to Jerusalem, but she chose to stay by herself at the back of the group.

The exhausted, excited group reached Jerusalem at sundown. Oil lamps on the tops of poles burned all across the city. Even Abbie agreed it was beautiful. They climbed the hill leading to the city. One of King David's men met them at the wide gate. He led Abbie's family to the most wonderful house she had ever seen. It was perched on the very top of the wall. Everyone exclaimed how happy they were to be in David's city. But Abbie wished King David had lost the battle for Jerusalem.

Father started a cooking fire. The bread dough they had carried with them was soon baking. Abbie didn't want to celebrate their first meal in their new home. She took an oil lamp to the sleeping room. There she found beds with legs on them. And on the floor was a red and purple woven rug.

I Wonder . . .
I wonder what needs to change before Abbie can enjoy all the new things . . .
I wonder if you've ever felt so sorry for yourself that you couldn't thank and praise God for all you have . . .

Blessed are those who have learned to shout praise to you. LORD, they live in the light of your favor.

Psalm 89:15

Escape

Abbie kneeled down on the rug, rubbing her hand across the soft material. "This rug is for you, Carmeline," she whispered. She rolled up the rug and tucked it under her arm. Then she curled up on a bed, planning her journey for tomorrow.

When the rest of the family came to the sleeping room, Mother whispered about how tired Abbie must have been. Father spoke in a quiet, sad voice back to Mother. "This is hard for Abbie. She has given so much to Carmeline and now . . ."

Abbie wanted to run into Father's arms. Didn't Father always understand? Didn't he always have a solution? She pinched herself. No, this time her plan was best.

Abbie kept herself awake through the night, hoping the rising sun would shine into the window of the new sleeping room. Even though she was ready for the morning, the brightness surprised her. The sunlight flooded the sleeping room, and when she stepped outside, she saw that the golden beams bathed the entire city.

It wasn't right that Father had forced her to run away. But since Father chose to obey the king, she was forced to disobey. Holding the rug close to her side, Abbie ran down the street to the gate. The guard at the gate stopped her, but she explained that she was meeting a friend who was on her way to the city. She told herself that it was a wish and not a lie. With the sun on her back, she turned left and went south into the Judean hills. After awhile it seemed as if the sun and the desert brown hills came together and circled around her. She stumbled. She was lost.

I Wonder . . .
I wonder why God wants you to obey and honor your parents . . .

"Honor your father and mother. Then you will live a long time in the land the LORD your God is giving you."

Exodus 20:12

The Meeting

The LORD trains those he loves. He is like a father who trains the son he is pleased with.

Proverbs 3:12

Abbie felt a cool wetness splashing over her lips and face. A man with features as craggy and brown as the hills stood over her.

"I told you. Leave that creature to die," called a woman from behind him. "If I can leave my children behind in Jerusalem, you can leave a stranger in the hills."

Abbie sat up and shivered in the heat. "What does she mean?"

"Never mind her," the man said. "We ran from Jerusalem to save our lives. Her husband killed himself over the capture of the city. Her son and daughter were gone—if she looked for them, there was a chance she'd get trapped or killed."

The panic of being separated from parents sent goose bumps across Abbie's arm. "Their names?" she asked. "I could look for her children in Jerusalem."

"Matin and Anoush," the man said. "But I doubt if they're alive."

The woman poked her finger into the man's chest. "Quit making friends. How often do I have to tell you? She looks like an Israelite—could even be a spy."

The harshness of the woman's words nearly caused Abbie to vomit. Her parents would never leave her somewhere. They'd risk their lives for her. She dropped her head. So what was she doing here? Carmeline didn't argue about staying in Hebron. Carmeline chose to obey her father and his calling to tend the fields of his fathers.

For the price of the rug the man pointed Abbie in the direction of Jerusalem. Then he disappeared into the hills with the woman.

Abbie hurried toward Jerusalem, knowing punishment awaited her. But so did love.

I Wonder...
I wonder in what ways God is like a parent who wants to care for you ...

The Fall of Jericho
Joshua 5:13-6:27

Have you ever played the trust game? If you have, you know how it goes: The teacher or leader blindfolds one person and chooses someone else to lead the blindfolded person. The blindfolded person has to listen as the guide explains when to step up or down and when to stop or go.

When the Israelites marched around the city of Jericho, it was something like the trust game. Even though they could see where they were going, they couldn't see any changes from day to day in the strong walls of Jericho. In their march they could do nothing except trust God and believe God would take care of what was coming next.

Proverbs 3: 5-6 helps you know the importance of putting your trust in God.

Litany	
Lambs	**Kids**
Trust in the LORD with all your heart.	
	Do not depend on your own understanding.
In all your ways remember him.	
	Then he will make your ways smooth and straight.

Song for the Week
"Trust and Obey," *Songs for LiFE* 213

Prayer for the Week
Lord, the stories in the Bible
show me that you should be trusted.
The people I know who love you
show me that you should be trusted.
So I want to remember all your ways.
I want to depend on you just like Joshua
and David and _____. Amen.

Passover

The setting sun glowed over Jerusalem as Abbie walked up the hill. The beauty of the city wasn't greater than last night, but this time it filled her with joy.

The gatekeeper stopped her. "The lost girl!" He blew the ram's horn trumpet. Between long and short blasts, streams of searchers returned from the valleys and mountains. "I found her!" he shouted.

Father was lengths ahead of the crowd. He scooped Abbie into his arms. "God saved you! I prayed you'd be found before our Passover supper."

Abbie had forgotten it was Passover, her favorite celebration. She loved the story of God rescuing the people from slavery in Egypt. But for the first time she realized God wanted to save her too. She untied her sandals. And danced barefoot. She knew that Carmeline would be celebrating in Hebron. The same God watched over both of them.

But somewhere in this city was a boy named Matin and a girl named Anoush—two who didn't know about the sacrifice of the lamb, two who didn't know God saved those who trusted in God as Lord. Did God have a plan for them?

As Abbie sat near the roasting lamb with her family, she told the story of the woman who abandoned her children.

The smoke from the fire curled around Father as he rotated the lamb. "That may explain the strange rustlings I heard in the house across from ours," he said. "Earlier I searched the house, thinking you might be there. I found nothing, but still I sensed someone was there."

I Wonder...

I wonder what amazes you most about God when you hear the stories of God's people escaping from Egypt, crossing the Red Sea, and watching the walls of Jericho tumble down . . .

Our people of long ago put their trust in you.

Psalm 22:4a

A Noise in the Night

As they feasted on the lamb and the unleavened bread, Abbie sat so she faced the house across the way. Without staring directly, she kept watch. More than once she had the sense that someone was watching from that rooftop. She hoped it wasn't her imagination. As she helped Mother with the cleanup, she wrapped leftover food into two bundles and placed them beside the warm ashes.

Mother said Abbie had had enough adventure for one day and had to go to bed. But it was impossible to sleep. Were the children older or younger than she was? If they were on their rooftop, did they see the food she left behind?

Late in the night, a lamb bleated in the shed below the house. A goat whinnied along with the lamb. Abbie swung her legs off the bed. Father and Mother were asleep. So was Jory.

It was a scary trip from the house high on the wall down to the courtyard, especially without a lamp. At the bottom doorway she darted to a post in the courtyard.

Under the light of the moon, Abbie saw two figures. They picked through the ashes of the evening fire. Didn't they see the food? It would frighten them if she went over to show them. If only the food were in her hands. Then she could hold out the bundles to show the children she wasn't an enemy.

Not far from Abbie was a clay jar of oranges. Placing one foot in front of another, she approached the stash of fruit. However, when she was only an arm's length away from the oranges, the two children slithered away into the darkness like frightened lizards.

I Wonder . . .
I wonder what would make Matin and Anoush afraid to trust Abbie . . .
I wonder what makes some people afraid to trust God . . .

> They trusted in you, and you didn't let them down.
>
> *Psalm 22:5b*

Abbie's Plan

In the morning after a meal of flat bread, honey, and goat's milk, Abbie told her parents about what she saw last night.

"Did they get any food?" Mother asked.

"No," Abbie said, "but we must build their trust by feeding them."

Mother agreed. She wrapped bundles of bread, figs, and oranges.

"It isn't enough," Abbie said. "They've been on their own since King David captured the city. What if they haven't had good food all this time?"

Mother filled two large baskets. "Do you want help carrying all this?" she asked.

"They might be scared of grown-ups," Abbie said.

Bent over from the weight of the baskets, she crossed the path. The gate to the courtyard opened as she leaned into it. She listened for footsteps or voices. There were none. She set the baskets on a bench.

For hours she waited outside the low courtyard wall. On the inside it was silent all morning. Not a sound came from the house or the courtyard. At noon, she slowly walked home. Had she been mistaken about the children living in that house?

"You did your best," Mother said.

"But it's not enough," Abbie said. "Please, may I search the streets?"

Mother sighed but let her go.

Before deciding which direction to take, Abbie peeked over the courtyard wall. The baskets were gone!

I Wonder...
I wonder if there's someone who trusts you because of your kindness . . .

Those who are poor will eat and be satisfied.

Psalm 22:26a

Rolling Apricots

Abbie squeezed herself. Matin and Anoush had to be inside the house after all. What could she tempt them with next? Without thinking about bringing silver coins, she hurried to the sellers' booths. A dark-skinned man displayed baskets of fragrant yellow-orange apricots. She offered her silver bracelets for the apricots. The bracelets were more valuable than the fruit, but she didn't mind about losing in the bargaining.

Excitedly, she ran back to the courtyard of Matin and Anoush's house. "Matin, Anoush," she called out. "Are you here?" There was no answer. She entered the house. The first room had a low table and plump cushions on the floor. Abbie's mind flashed back to the woman in the Judean hills—Matin and Anoush's mother. Should she tell Matin and Anoush what happened to their father? Should she explain that their mother would most likely never return?

She paused at the bottom of the stone steps that led to the second floor. Then she climbed slowly, cautiously to the top.

In the corner of the upstairs room a boy and girl huddled together. The boy's face was misshapen, and the girl's eyes were dark and haunting.

"I—I want to help," Abbie said.

"Then go away and don't tell anyone we are here," the boy said. "If we are found, we will die."

The desperation in Matin's voice made Abbie back up. But before she left, she rolled an apricot to Anoush. Abbie thought she saw a quick flash of a smile.

Those who look to the LORD will praise him. May their hearts be filled with new hope!

Psalm 22:26b

I Wonder . . .
I wonder why it's hard to trust someone when you're scared . . .

New Owners

Abbie left Matin and Anoush. Plans raced through Abbie's head as she ran up the steps to her tower home.

"There she is," voices shouted at her.

At first Abbie was confused. Then she realized her best friend, Carmeline, was standing in her home. "Are you visiting?" She finally managed to say.

Carmeline giggled. "My father's new duty is the chief overseer of King David's fields. My uncle returned to Hebron, so he can take the family fields."

A great sense of joy and relief flowed over Abbie. She almost cried. But inside her plans suddenly grew larger. She and Carmeline were a team that got things done.

"And best of all," Carmeline said, "King David has assigned us the house just across from you. We will live next to each other just as we always said we would."

Abbie's heart nearly stopped. Matin and Anoush's house! "But—but you can't!"

Abbie's parents' eyes opened wide. Carmeline and her parents stared at Abbie.

There was no way to protect Matin and Anoush. Tears streamed down her face as she told the story.

Carmeline's mother kneeled beside Abbie. "My dear Abbie, this is a miracle. My husband is bringing the firstfruits of the fields to King David. But what about my desire to mother more children after my two babies died? Could it be possible these children are to come under my care?"

Abbie felt as if she had wings. God had a plan after all!

I Wonder...

I wonder what Abbie meant when she said, "God had a plan after all"...

All the rich people of the earth will worship God and take part in his feasts.

Psalm 22:29a

Deborah and Jael

Judges 4-5

What kinds of people do you think God chooses to serve him? People who have studied the Bible for a long time? People who are wealthy and important?

The Bible shows us that sometimes God chooses the people we least expect.

In this week's Bible story, Jael was that person. Jael was just an ordinary person—not someone important or well known. But those things don't matter to God. God doesn't care who your family is, how old you are, or whether you are a girl or a boy. God chooses those who are willing to be brave and serve God, those who are honest and faithful.

This week, repeat these words from Psalm 37:28, 30.

Litany	
Lambs	**Kids**
The LORD loves those who are honest.	
	He will not desert those who are faithful to him.
The mouths of those who do what is right speak words of wisdom.	
	They say what is honest.

Song for the Week
"¡Canta, Débora, Canta!" *Songs for LiFE* 107

Prayer for the Week
Dear Lord, not enough people to fill a gym
even know my name.
But I want to be ready if you call
me to do something.
If I can be faithful to do the right things
where I am, then I am faithful to you. Amen.

A Dare

I love you, LORD.
You give me
strength.

Psalm 18:1

Jory touched his first two fingers to his lips. Then he placed those fingers on the metal box that hung on the doorframe. It was the same box they had in Hebron. Inside were written the words of God, reminding Jory and his family to always love God (see Deut. 6:4-9).

Before they moved to Jerusalem, Jory sometimes forgot to touch the box on his way out to play. But now that he was living in the great city of David, obeying the ways of God, the king, and his father was more exciting.

Hezro walked by just as Jory took his fingers off the box. "Look at the good little boy," Hezro said.

Jory felt his face becoming warm. "My father says a strong Israelite never forgets his daily promise to God."

Hezro laughed. "Do you always do what your father says?"

Jory nodded.

"Well." Hezro rubbed the wool square of his slingshot. "A boy has to become a man someday—do things on his own."

More than anything Jory dreamed of the day when Father would say, "Jory has the heart and mind of a man."

Hezro twirled his slingshot. "So do you want to explore the city with me? Maybe even scare away a Jebusite boy I saw lurking around."

"I'm spending the day with Father at the gate," Jory said.

"That's right." Hezro stopped the twirling. "You're Daddy's little boy."

I Wonder . . .
I wonder if you have times when it's not so easy to obey God and your parents . . .

The Adventure

Jory watched Hezro walk away. What would be the harm in an adventure? Discovering the city had its advantages. And if there was a Jebusite worshiping false gods or doing other things against God's law, the king should be informed.

"Wait up, Hezro. I'm with you."

Hezro slapped him on the shoulders. "You won't be sorry. Did your father ever tell you how David's commander, Joab, broke into the city?"

"Yes," Jory said, "through a tunnel under the city. He climbed a shaft that no one had attempted before. It was a daring feat."

"Let's explore the tunnel," Hezro said. "But we'd better check it from the inside. If we go outside the city, we'll pass by your father at the gate."

Jory paused. If Hezro thought this adventure was a good thing, why did they have to be sneaky? But Hezro was already running toward the tunnel.

By the time Jory caught up, Hezro had entered the tunnel. Oil lamps flickered all along the dark path. It was an adventure just being down under the earth.

"Hurry," Hezro called. "The shaft is up ahead."

As the boys stood over the hole in the tunnel floor, Hezro dropped a stone. They had time to look at each other before they heard the faint plunk in the water below.

"It was a powerful amount of water that cut through this stone," Hezro said.

Jory agreed, but he also thought it was a mighty God who brought Joab and his men up from the bottom. How many times did God help people with the impossible?

I Wonder . . .

I wonder if you can think of a time when God led someone you know to a safe place . . .

He brought me out into a wide and safe place. He saved me because he was pleased with me.

Psalm 18:19

Deep Trouble

When I was
in trouble . . .
I cried to my
God for help.

Psalm 18:6

Jory flopped on his belly next to the opening. He stretched his arm down the shaft.

"Do you want to go down?" Hezro asked.

"No," Jory said. "The smooth, wet sides are too slippery."

"I'm going down then. If I get stuck, throw me the water bucket rope and pull me back up."

Jory's mouth dropped open. "You're twice my size. I couldn't lift you a digit."

Hezro flexed his arm muscles. "I could do it—I mean pull you up. So I guess you'll have to be the one to go down. There must be uneven places you can grip with your feet and hands."

"It's dark, though."

"You're not afraid, are you?" Hezro asked.

Jory took a deep breath. He couldn't let Hezro see his fear. "Okay, I'll go."

He flipped over so his feet hung over the shaft's opening. Hezro gripped Jory's hands. Then Hezro eased Jory down into the darkness. When the edge was level with Jory's neck, Jory called, "Pull me up."

"Search with your feet for a ledge," Hezro said as he lowered Jory a head length more. It was as far as Hezro could go without falling in himself.

"My toe hit something," Jory said.

"Good," called out Hezro. Then he let go.

As Jory's foot balanced on a narrow ledge, he spread his arms and hugged the rock wall. What next? He was afraid to move.

I Wonder . . .
I wonder if God helps us even when we cause our own troubles . . .

Where Is Hezro?

"Hezro," called Jory. "I can't move."

"Let your foot drop until you reach another ledge," Hezro called down. "If you keep doing that, you'll get to the bottom."

Jory's body trembled just thinking about moving his foot. What would Father do? Pray. Yes, Father would pray. Closing his eyes and talking to God stopped his trembling. Then he heard a voice that wasn't Hezro's. Surely this person would help or convince Hezro to pull out a stuck boy. He kissed the wet stone wall.

"Psst, Jory," Hezro called down. "That Jebusite boy I saw yesterday is here. He'll want to know what I am doing, so I better leave. If you're quiet, he won't realize you are down there."

It was bad enough being stuck when someone was up there, aware of his troubles. But now what?

"Send someone to save me," he prayed. Would it be Father? No, Father had to guard the gate until sundown. Jory wondered if he could hold on that long. Perhaps Hezro would tell someone. No, he'd be foolish to ever believe in the goodness of Hezro again.

For the third time Jory prayed. "Lord, do you see me down here? Show me what to do." He rested his cheek against the cold stone. The words from the scroll in the metal box flashed in his mind—"Love God with all your strength."

Never give up, he reminded himself. Not your grip, not your love for God.

I Wonder . . .

I wonder if it is easy to give up when things get really tough . . .

I wonder how you stay strong when troubles come . . .

The LORD is my rock and my fort. He is the One who saves me.

Psalm 18:2

Tarik

"Hello," called a voice. "Do you need help?"

The way the boy said his words told Jory he was the Jebusite. Would God send a Jebusite to help him? Jory breathed slowly and deeply.

"I have advice for you," the Jebusite yelled. "Soon the Gihon spring will gush all the way from the bottom to where you are."

The rock sides felt slipperier than before. Water sputtered at the bottom.

He had no choice but to depend on the Jebusite. "What should I do?" he called.

"I come down here almost every day," the boy said. "I watch the gushing water. And I wonder what it would be like to ride the great white fountain. Well now, you don't have a choice. Get ready to hold your breath. Then when the gusher rises, curl into a ball and drop into it. Don't fight it. As it slows, enjoy the ride to the bottom."

There wasn't time to think. Jory rolled into the hand of the water. Then after many long choppy burps, it bounced him down to the bottom of the water tunnel.

A boy stretched out his hand to Jory. "I'm Tarik, the one who told you to ride the gusher. I ran as fast as I could to meet you. Was it fun?"

Jory laughed and cried at the same time. "The Lord sent you to save me."

"The Lord?" Tarik asked. "The God of King David?"

Jory nodded.

"It's your God that fascinates me," Tarik said. "For days I've been looking for someone to tell me about your God."

I Wonder . . .

I wonder what is the very first thing you would tell Tarik about God . . .

LORD, to those who are faithful you show that you are faithful.

Psalm 18:25a

Gideon
Judges 6-7

What are you sure of? Your favorite foods? The person you want for your best friend? How to find your house? Most likely your list will include things you can see, touch, taste, smell, or hear. Your five senses let you know what is real.

In this week's Bible story, Gideon wanted a little help from his senses. If he could see or touch something from God, he could be sure that God called him.

You can't touch God. Yet God wants you to know the strength that belongs to your Lord. The Bible uses rocks and forts to picture God. You can touch them and know they are strong. And they won't go away. This week use Psalm 31:2b-3 to think of God as your rock and fort.

Litany	
Lambs	**Kids**
Be the rock I go to for safety.	
	Be the strong fort that saves me.
You are my rock and my fort.	
	Lead me and guide me for the honor of your name.

Song for the Week
"Protect Me, God: I Trust in You," *Songs for LiFE* 217

Prayer for the Week
Lord, sometimes I like to climb big rocks.
I'm never afraid that the rock will crumble underneath me.
As I play and work, let me know I can stand on your promises.
I will think about how strong you are. Amen.

Royal Treatment

God's people who live in our land are glorious. I take great delight in them.

Psalm 16:3

Tarik and Jory scrambled out of the tunnel. Their clothes were wet.

"There's a large, smooth rock on the mountain," Tarik said. "Let's climb up there and dry out in the sun."

As the boys stretched out their legs on the rock, Tarik compared his legs to Jory's. They were the same length. Would Jory become his best friend?

From their spot high up on the mountain they could see over the wall of the city. People were hurrying about, patching weak spots on the roofs of the houses, replacing stones in the wall of the fort, and dumping broken idol pieces over the south wall.

Tarik's eyes searched for his house. It was quiet, and Tarik knew why. His family was afraid to come out and work with the Israelites.

"What kind of a king is David?" Tarik asked. "Is he a fair king?"

"Well, he does have favorites," Jory said. "He treats God's people like princes."

Tarik reached out his hand to a lizard that poked its head up next to the rock. But the lizard was smart. It got away. Is that what his family should do? They were hiding in their house because they didn't want to move his ill sister. But they weren't God's people or King David's favorites. A king got rid of those he didn't like.

Jory jumped off the rock. He caught the lizard.

Tarik touched the twitching tail of the little creature. Then he made up his mind. He must convince his family to stay and learn the ways of God and the king. That was the only way.

I Wonder . . .

I wonder if you know someone who wants to learn more about God's ways . . .

I wonder if you can help . . .

Who Does the King Know?

Tarik asked Jory to teach him about God. So Jory told his favorite stories—the ones about Gideon and Rahab. Tarik decided that if Rahab could become one of God's people, so could anyone who believed. Even Tarik and his family. And he liked the answers God gave to Gideon's tests.

Tarik said goodbye to Jory so he could tell his family the stories. Hopping over red field lilies, he ran down the mountain and into Jerusalem.

His father was waiting for him in the courtyard of their home. "We must take our oxen to market and trade them for food."

Tarik saw his father's stonemason equipment in the wooden-wheeled wagon. "If you sell the oxen, how will you get your stones from the hills and fields?"

"This is a new kingdom, son. A king has his own stonemasons."

"But Father, you're the best."

"The king doesn't know that," Father said.

Tarik thought of Rahab and Gideon. "The God of Israel will help us," he said. "The king will trust a stonemason who depends on God."

Father shook his head. "Their God isn't our god. And the king doesn't know me or my work. There isn't even anyone to tell him about me."

"I can tell you about God," Tarik said, lifting his head to look into his father's dark eyes. He didn't see a spark of excitement jump into Father's eyes. He wanted Father to understand God's ability. "Maybe God will give us a sign that we can be his people too," he said. "If the king gives you a stonemason job, will you trust that God will care for us in Jerusalem?"

I Wonder...
I wonder what signs of God's care you see in your life . . .

LORD . . . Save me because you do what is right.

Psalm 31:1

A New Palace

LORD . . . pay
attention to me.

Psalm 31:1a, 2a

Tarik skipped and sang on the way to see King David. Father carried his hammer with the toothed edge. It was used for shaping stones. This hammer would prove to the king that Father was a skilled stonemason. Tarik begged Father to take one of the large stones he had shaped and smoothed, but Father said it was too much. The worst part was that Father walked slowly, as if there were no job waiting for him. Finally they reached the fort where King David lived.

"See how high the fort is," Father said. "It protects the king from people like us. No one can even reach the king unless the guards take you inside."

Tarik allowed his gaze to travel all the way to the top of the fort. It was true that no one was protected like the king. Except . . . hadn't Jory said that God was like a fort protecting those who trusted God as Lord?

Many workers stretched over the rock hill that safeguarded the fort. The king hired these workers. They were making the city of Jerusalem great again. One more worker should help the king's plans to go faster.

Tarik took Father's toothed-edged hammer and walked in front of a guard.

"Where did you get that tool?" asked the guard.

"It's my father's. He is the best stonemason in the city."

"You don't say," the guard said. "Does your father know that King David is preparing to build a new palace?"

I Wonder . . .
I wonder if you can think of one (or maybe more!) way that God is like a fort . . .

Outside the King's Fort

Tarik called Father to meet the guard.

"This is my father," Tarik said. "He has a plumb line and a measuring reed too."

The guard scowled when Father offered his hand.

"You a Jebusite?" asked the guard.

Father nodded.

The guard moved away from the fort as if to say he didn't want Tarik and Father any closer to the king. "How do I know if you are trustworthy?" asked the guard. He pointed to a rubbish pile of broken, chipped stones. "Or how do I know your work is straight and even?" Then he turned his back on them.

"Let's go home, Father. We'll get your best work and bring it back to him. Then he'll give you a chance."

"No," Father said. "We are going home to pack. We will leave the city with your mother and sisters. The answer to the test is that we do not belong in Jerusalem and God is not our god."

Tarik thought about it when he sat on the rock next to Jory. Why did he feel so strong when Jory was telling the stories and now feel so weak? He had brought God's name to Father. Didn't God want Father to believe?

A gentle breeze danced through a palm branch, but it seemed more like a day when the wind blew so hard that the strong trees bent and broke.

I Wonder . . .
I wonder how God works in people's hearts to help them believe . . .

[LORD], Lead me and guide me for the honor of your name.

Psalm 31:3b

A Different Test

"Father," Tarik said, "perhaps we asked the wrong guard. We can't walk away from the greatest God because of that guard."

Father put his hand on Tarik's shoulder. "I've never seen you so strong about something. It almost makes me believe in this God."

Tarik's heart leaped. But before they found another guard, the first one came back to them.

"I'll give you an opportunity," he said. "In the city there lives a man whose opinion the king values. If that man can speak honorably about you, the king will hire you." The guard scratched lines on a broken pottery piece. "Follow this path to the man's house."

Tarik sighed. He had asked God to give a sign to his father. But how could that ever happen if they had to pass the guard's test? It seemed impossible. What great man respected by the king would give his word of approval to complete strangers?

Father headed in the direction of the wise man's house. This time Tarik didn't think he could get his feet to move. But for Father's sake he kept up. They stopped at the house that the guard's map had directed them to.

Father knocked. A boy opened the door. It was Jory!

"You came!" Jory said. "I was just wishing I had told you how to find my house. My father wants to meet the boy who saved my life. And meet his family too."

I Wonder . . .
I wonder if you see a sign from God in today's story . . .

Into your hands I commit my very life. LORD, set me free. You are my faithful God.

Psalm 31:5

Samson

Judges 13-16

D o your outside and inside match?

That might sound like a strange question. But just as you choose what you will wear on the outside each day, you also choose what you will "wear" on the inside.

Samson's choice for the outside was never to have his hair cut. In his day, that told people he was committed to pure living. But what Samson chose for the outside didn't match what he chose for the inside.

This week and always, think about what you are wearing on the inside as well as the outside. Proverbs 3:3-4 has some good advice about choosing the right things to wear on the inside.

Litany	
Lambs	**Kids**
Don't let love and truth ever leave you.	
	Tie them around your neck.
Write them on the tablet of your heart.	
	Then you will find favor and a good name in the eyes of God and people.

Song for the Week
"Psalm 51," *Songs for LiFE* 41

Prayer for the Week
Lord, sometimes I put the wrong things in my heart.
Doing that is worse than wearing dirty jeans to school.
Clean me up. Dress my heart in the pure white of your Holy Spirit.
Then my spirit will be faithful to you. Amen.

Gold and Jewels

Ronia draped a gold chain over her forehead. Then she looked into the polished copper mirror. She sighed. Without a jewel to wear on her forehead, she wasn't as beautiful as the queen. Ronia removed the shiny chain. She needed a red sparkling ruby like the one Abigail, King David's wife, wore. Just today Ronia had seen the queen wearing the jewel on her forehead. And more than anything Ronia wanted to copy the queen.

The bracelets on Ronia's arm tinkled against each other. Father, who was the king's treasurer, had given them to her. He promised her that the bracelets were as fine as the ones the king gave to Abigail.

She skipped into the courtyard where Father was eating his morning bread. She leaned over and kissed the tip of Father's beard.

"Abigail has a beautiful red stone," Ronia said. "She wears it every day. I want one too. Then you can be proud that your daughter is as lovely as a queen."

Father pushed Ronia away. "The jewels are too precious. There aren't enough for you to have one."

"All I need is a little one, Father. Surely you have a tiny sparkling stone in the treasure house. You always say the king wants you and your family to be happy." She batted her eyelids. "I'll go with you today and find one."

Father threw down his bread. Then he said, "It's not a good day for you to come. I have important business with a man today."

Ronia stuck out her lower lip. It wasn't fair. How could she get Father to change his mind? "Abbie and Carmeline can go with their fathers any time they want," she said.

Father didn't say anything. He tied his sandals and walked out the courtyard gate.

"Why are you so mean?" she called after him.

I Wonder . . .
I wonder if wanting more than you have could cause trouble in your family . . .

Anyone who always wants more brings trouble to his family.

Proverbs 15:27

A Storehouse of Treasures

After Father was gone, Ronia stomped up to the rooftop. It wasn't true that Abbie and Carmeline could go with their fathers any time. But it was true that Abbie and Carmeline played pretend games about being the queen. Ronia thought her dresses and bracelets were most like the queen's, so she should always be chosen. But the other girls said they had to take turns. Ronia imagined appearing in front of Abbie and Carmeline with a jewel on her head like Abigail's. Then her friends would have to choose her as the queen every time.

Mother came up to the rooftop, interrupting Ronia's daydreaming.

"Have you seen Father?" Mother asked. "I'm afraid he left this morning without a fresh piece of damp clay. He'll need it for recording new amounts of silver today."

Ronia jumped to her feet. "Yes, he did leave. But I can bring him the clay." She checked her appearance in the bronze mirror and then left for the treasure house with the lump of clay.

When she arrived, the large, heavy door wasn't bolted. She opened the door a crack and squeezed inside. The thick stone walls of the building blocked the outside light, but dozens of flickering oil lamps reflected light on the gold and silver objects in the room. Father was talking to a man dressed in a long purple robe. Bags of silver sat on the floor between the two men. Father had important business after all. She stood still, hoping to go unnoticed. But it was too late.

"Go to the next room," Father said. "And don't come out until I call you."

She dropped the clay on Father's table and stumbled into a dim room under the first arch.

I Wonder . . .

I wonder how you feel when you get yourself into trouble . . .
I wonder what you should do about it . . .

Hard training is in store for anyone who leaves the right path.

Proverbs 15:10a

Borrowed

A thin trail of smoke rose from a single lamp. Swords of all sizes and bronze shields filled this room. It reminded Ronia of a battlefield. She shivered, thinking about fighting soldiers. Then she noticed a faint light coming from a side room. Following the direction of the light led her to a short and narrow passageway. She wriggled through it into a small low-ceilinged room. On a ledge stood a large oil lamp. Next to the lamp, colored sparks reflected the light's flame. Jewels! There were many colors—bright red, green, and yellow. Only one of the stones had a gold edge and a gold hook for a chain. It was a large red one—one that was like Abigail's.

Ronia held it in her hand. The sparkle of the stones hidden away in this special room helped Ronia understand what Father meant about the jewels being very valuable. But it was hard to put the red stone back. It was easier to imagine showing it to Abbie and Carmeline and impressing them.

What if she just borrowed the stone? She could return it tomorrow. Father would never know. She tucked the ruby into the folds of her belt. Then without looking back she left the small room. The weapons room made Ronia more nervous than it had earlier. But she told herself to wait until Father came.

"Ronia." It was Father. "What did you see while you were here?"

"Just some swords and shields."

Father clenched his fist. "Go home now. It'll be a long time before I allow you to return."

I Wonder . . .
I wonder what Ronia will do with the ruby . . .
I wonder why one trouble often grows into bigger troubles . . .

It is better to have respect for the LORD and have little than to be rich and have trouble.

Proverbs 15:16

The Wise and Beautiful Abigail

Ronia ran from the storehouse, running until she couldn't take another step. The inside of her head pounded so hard she didn't even know where she was.

Then she heard her name.

Abbie and Carmeline called to her from a rooftop.

"Is something wrong?" Abbie shouted. "You look as if you're running from danger."

Ronia took a deep breath. She needed an excuse. "Yes," she said. "There was a strange man with a sword. But I think I lost him."

"Go through the gate and come up here," Carmeline said.

Ronia paused at the gate. She was sweaty and dusty from running through the streets. It wasn't how she wanted to impress Carmeline and Abbie with queen-like ways. But she was thirsty and, no matter what, she could trust the girls to give her a drink.

When she reached the rooftop she discovered the girls were not alone. At least ten others were there. Carmeline and Abbie had spread out a feast of bread and fresh goat's milk.

"What are you celebrating?" Ronia asked, wondering why she hadn't been invited.

Abbie walked elegantly over to Ronia with a tray of food. "We are pretending to be Abigail. Remember how she fed all of David's soldiers? We don't have raisin cakes or sweet fig cakes, but we are being generous with what we have."

Carmeline had simple red flowers in her hair instead of jewels. "King David loved Abigail because of her wisdom and beauty. Someday I'll be as wise as Abigail."

Ronia's stomach hurt. She wasn't one bit wise and she certainly didn't feel beautiful.

The eyes of the LORD are everywhere. They watch those who are evil and those who are good.

Proverbs 15:3

I Wonder . . .
I wonder why the girls admired Abigail . . .
Read the Bible story about Abigail in 1 Samuel 25:1-42.

Caught

Ronia touched the ruby between the folds of her belt. A person like Abigail would be more likely to give away a jewel than to steal one. Ronia decided that returning the ruby was the right thing to do, even if it meant telling Father the awful truth. She excused herself from the party.

All the way to the storehouse her heart thumped. When she got there, loud voices echoed from the main room. Ronia stood rigid outside the door. Soon the door swung open. Two soldiers dragged Father out of the building.

"My daughter," called Father.

The soldiers pushed Father forward. The man in the long purple robe Ronia had seen earlier that morning stopped beside Ronia. "I'm sorry to bring you bad news," he said, "but your father is a thief."

The ruby, thought Ronia. They think Father stole it. She dug her fingers into the folds of the belt, brought out the red stone, and handed it to the man. "It was me. I stole the ruby."

The man shook his head. "You? So I suppose it was true that your father knew nothing about the missing ruby."

Ronia hiccuped sobs. "You can free Father now."

Great sadness covered the man's face. "Your father is still a thief. He has been stealing from the king for a long time. It wasn't until this morning that I could prove it. I pretended to be a wealthy man honoring the king, but actually I work for him. I gave your father ten bags of silver, but when the report came back to the palace only seven were listed."

All the silver and gold that Father used so freely from the treasure house suddenly made sense. "Will we go to prison?" she asked.

The man held her hand. "I'll take you to Abigail. She'll know what to do about you. And the king will judge your father."

The houses of those who do what is right hold great wealth. But those who do what is wrong earn only trouble.

Proverbs 15:6

I Wonder . . .
I wonder if Ronia should be punished . . .
I wonder in what ways stealing hurts others and God . . .

Ruth
Book of Ruth

Once there was a girl who went to the park without getting permission. Her dog saw her leave and followed her. While she was there, she fell from the crossbars. Her leg hurt too much to move. That's when her dog took action. He ran home, barking. He didn't stop barking until the family followed him to the park. They carried their daughter home. And because the dog had followed the girl and watched over her, they gave the dog a new name. From that time forward he was called Goodness.

Goodness followed Ruth too. God didn't send goodness through a dog, but he sent it through Boaz and the blessings of a child and a great-grandchild—the one who became the great king of Israel, David.

Psalm 23:6 and Psalm 27:13 tell you that the Lord's goodness is there for you.

Litany	
Lambs	**Kids**
I'm sure that your goodness and love will follow me.	
	I will see the LORD's goodness.
I'm sure that your goodness and love will follow me.	
	I will see the LORD's goodness.

Song for the Week
"Go Now in Peace," *Songs for LiFE* 79

Prayer for the Week
Lord, how good you are.
Even when I'm not thinking about you,
you are there, watching, protecting,
shining your love on me. Amen.

Raisins

God, you know
how foolish I've
been. My guilt
is not hidden
from you.

Psalm 69:5

Ronia's father went to prison. Their home was sold to another family. But Ronia and her mother and brother didn't have to live in the street. The queen gave them servant jobs and servant rooms in the new palace of King David.

Three days before the king's first banquet in the new palace, Ronia was up to her elbows in raisins. She sorted one raisin at a time, removing the stems and dried leaves that didn't belong.

"Chin-up," called a boy delivering another wheeled cart of raisins. He spilled them onto Ronia's work place. "That's all," he said.

Ronia gave him a shy smile.

He walked away. Then he came back. "Don't I know you?"

Clumps of sticky raisins held fast to Ronia's fingers. The boy was familiar to her too. He was the son of an important family in the city. But she wasn't ready to tell him that she was Ronia, the daughter of Uri, who was in prison for stealing. Or that she had also stolen.

"I'll tell you my name," he said. "I'm Jehesah. My father is one of the king's musicians. Someday I'll be a musician too. Now you have to tell me your name."

"Raisin girl," Ronia said.

"No, tell me your real name," Jehesah pleaded.

"First tell me why you are delivering raisins and not working on your music."

Jehesah sighed. "My music isn't good enough to play with the adults for the king's banquet. So I sneaked in with the delivery boy's cart—just for a peek at the palace."

Ronia dug her hands deep into the raisins. She longed to have a friend like Jehesah. But all the mistakes in her past would keep that from happening.

I Wonder . . .

I wonder why Ronia is afraid to tell Jehesah who she is . . .

A Favor

Ronia carried a large bowl of sorted raisins over to a pot of honey. It put a little distance between her and Jehesah. At least for a while.

Jehesah picked a stem off a raisin. Then another. Silently Ronia went back to work beside her new partner.

After the raisin pile leveled down to the height of Ronia's waist, Jehesah stopped.

"You're not a very talkative girl," he said. "What's wrong with you?"

"You mean what's wrong with *you?*" Ronia said. "If you'd go home and work on your music, you might be invited to the palace the next time."

Jehesah threw his hands into the air. Then he marched out of the palace kitchen.

After he left, Ronia fought back her tears. It was impossible to see brown stems on brown raisins with tears in her eyes. Why did Jehesah have to come anyway? It only made her see once again that she didn't know how to be a friend.

"Say, girlie," the cook said. "Where did your friend go?"

"I don't have any friends," Ronia said.

The cook dusted flour into the air as she raised her arms. "Better talk to God about that."

Ronia picked up the bowl of raisins that Jehesah had sorted. The raisins smelled sweet. For the first time they weren't a sticky brown mess. Could the sticky mess with her friends ever be sweet? She bowed her head. Before she finished her prayer, she had an idea.

I Wonder . . .
I wonder if talking to God is a little like talking to a friend . . .

But LORD, I pray to you. May this be the time you show me your favor.

Psalm 69:13a

For a Friend

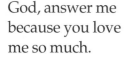

God, answer me
because you love
me so much.

Psalm 69:13b

As Ronia finished sorting the raisins, she worked on a plan. But there wasn't much time. Tomorrow she had to make the raisin cakes. The following day was the king's banquet. The palace would be overflowing with guests. But none of those guests would be those her age or younger—unless she could get a special invitation for them. On her way out of the kitchen she looked up and down the hallway. Every evening she had obediently turned left to the small room she shared with the other servant girls. But far down the hall to the right and past the flowering gardens were the rooms belonging to the queen. She turned right.

Each step that brought her closer made her more afraid. She had worked hard for two months, but she didn't deserve any special favors from the queen. Before assigning Ronia to the kitchen, though, the queen had said. "I pray that goodness may be with you." And in the queen's beautiful eyes Ronia thought she saw love.

"Who goes there?" called a voice from behind Ronia.

Ronia threw herself against the wall. But she couldn't escape from the woman servant who saw her.

"You don't belong down here," the queen's maiden said.

"I . . . I know," Ronia said. "I was just hoping that . . . "

The maiden stared at Ronia. "Aren't you the girl the queen sent to the kitchen?"

Ronia nodded. "I'm sorry. I wanted to ask the queen a favor, but I don't deserve any extra kindness."

I Wonder . . .
I wonder if you've ever asked God for something you never expected to happen . . .

Good News

Ronia wished she could escape the gaze and questions of the servant. "The queen asked about you yesterday," the maiden servant said. "She wanted to make sure you were living honestly. I gave her a good report. And she was pleased."

Ronia dropped her head. She had hoped that someday the queen would notice her good work. And now that she had, was it all lost?

"So what is the favor you want to ask the queen?" asked the maiden servant.

Ronia didn't dare speak.

"Don't be afraid," the servant said.

"The banquet tomorrow," Ronia said. "Could those who are twelve and under be invited? It would be special for my friends. I mean . . . it would be nice for those who would like to come."

The servant maiden nodded. Ronia thought she saw a bit of a smile.

"I'll ask the queen," the servant said. "Now you better go to your side of the palace before someone else catches you."

Ronia did as she was told. The other servant girls in her room giggled and talked about the banquet throughout the evening, but Ronia stared at the ceiling. Would the queen think kindly of the idea?

Early in the morning on the way to the kitchen, the maiden servant stopped Ronia. "I have good news," she said. "You may invite anyone you want. Go now and tell them."

I Wonder . . .
I wonder if God's kindness to you has ever taken you by surprise . . .

LORD, answer me because your love is so good. Turn to me because you are so kind.

Psalm 69:16

Goodness

I will praise God's name by singing to him. I will bring him glory by giving thanks.

Psalm 69:30

Ronia picked at a raisin stuck to her tunic. "Who will believe a kitchen girl is inviting them?" she mumbled.

"You do look miserable," the servant said. "Wait here. I'll get you new clothes."

The servant returned with an armful of clothes and jewels. "Keep it all," she said.

The soft fabrics brushed against Ronia's cheek as the servant placed the clothes in Ronia's arms. Then the servant left.

Ronia pictured herself going to Abbie's house and showing off the beautiful clothes. Her old pride was back. How could that happen so quickly? It made her sad about herself. She had to prove that she was different than before.

Forgetting about her brown-stained fingers, her bare feet, and the hairs that strayed from her braid, she left the palace to find Abbie and Carmeline.

At Abbie's house the girls sat on the low wall surrounding the courtyard. She waved at them. They didn't wave back. How could she have been so foolish? She ran. But she didn't get far before Abbie and Carmeline caught up with her.

"Ronia," Carmeline said, "we didn't recognize you at first. Do you have a free day?"

Ronia gulped. It sounded as if they knew everything about her situation. So why were they even talking to her?

"We've thought about you every day," Carmeline said. "We've asked the Lord of all good things to bless you."

The kind words made Ronia feel braver. "I've come with news from the queen," she said. "You are invited to the banquet. Tell all your friends."

Abbie and Carmeline clapped.

Ronia thought about the dresses from the servant. There'd be one for each of them. But that surprise would have to wait until tomorrow. It was time to invite Jehesah.

I Wonder . . .
I wonder if you've ever felt so thankful you wanted to dance and sing . . .

Hannah Prays

1 Samuel 1-2:10

Sometimes life is like getting an ordinary-size box for your birthday when you were wishing for a bicycle. That dream bike would have meant the other kids would no longer laugh at you for riding a tricycle. But then, when you open the too-small box you discover a helmet that goes along with the bike waiting in the garage!

Hannah wished for children. In her day, a married woman who had no children was looked down upon. God listened to Hannah's sorrow. And God made her dream of being a mother come true. Hannah's first child brought her from the bottom to the top.

Because life brings more ups and downs than dream bikes, the words of Hannah in 1 Samuel 2:7-8 remind you that God plans good for you. It may not always be what you expect, and the wait may be long, but you can always trust in God.

Litany	
Lambs	**Kids**
The LORD lifts people up.	
	He raises poor people up from the trash pile.
He lets them sit with princes.	
	He gives them places of honor.

Song for the Week
"All Good Gifts Around Us," *Songs for LiFE* 69

Prayer for the Week
Lord, in my waiting
may I always wait on you.
You never give up on me.
Your plan for me is perfect.
I look forward to what will come from your hand. Amen.

Not for Matin?

Matin decided that every day was a celebration. That is, every day since Gareb and Zenda had adopted him and Anoush. Matin still couldn't bring himself to call them Father and Mother though. All his life he had thought that a mother and father were there to punish, not to love. Now he watched Carmeline run to her parents with her troubles. If only he could open up his heart like that. At least for Anoush it was easier. She hugged Zenda when she was happy and when she was sad.

Matin never asked for anything. But he never lacked new things. When Gareb and Zenda gave him the new crutch—the one that was the right length for his growing body, he said thank you by digging up a flower in the field and putting it in a pot for Zenda. And that became his pattern. They had the most colorful courtyard in all of Jerusalem. Only King David's gardens could compare with theirs.

For every new blossom that appeared on a plant, Matin gave thanks to God. This family wasn't going to leave him. And bit by bit he started believing that this God was going to be the same way. "God will be better to you than I can be," his new father said. Matin smiled, trying to imagine that.

But the news Carmeline brought today scared him back to the old days. "We're invited to the king's banquet," she said. "You and I and Anoush and all our friends. We'll see the king, eat his food, and walk through his garden."

Matin's whole body felt as lame as his leg. The words from David's commander, Joab, echoed in his head—"Blind and disabled people will never be welcomed in David's palace."

I Wonder . . .
I wonder if you think Matin would be welcome at King David's party . . .

LORD, you are mighty. You are faithful in everything you do.

Psalm 89:8b

Sick

Matin gazed in the direction of the new palace. There had never been a finer building in all of Jerusalem. Beautiful gifts from far-away lands filled this palace, and Matin longed to see them.

But Matin was sure that if Joab or one of his men saw Matin in the palace, they'd throw him out. When soldiers make promises, they don't go back on them.

If only he could run to Gareb the way Carmeline did. Gareb did everything he could to help Matin walk straighter and stronger. But what would Gareb say if he knew about Joab's words against the blind and the disabled? Would Gareb start thinking that he didn't want a lame son?

At the evening meal, Matin was so filled with his sorrow that it was hard to swallow. He had to invent an excuse for not going to the banquet.

"Matin," Mother said, "where is your big appetite?"

"I'm not feeling well," he said. Then it entered his mind. That's what he could say tomorrow morning too.

Zenda came over. She put her hand on his head. "You do feel a bit warm. Why don't you go to bed early so that in the morning you'll feel well enough for the banquet."

In the morning, Mother Zenda kneeled beside his bed. "How are you doing?"

Matin moaned. "Worse," he said. "I'd like to stay in bed. Is that okay?"

Mother Zenda rubbed his arms. "I don't want you to miss out on the good times."

"There'll be more good times," Matin said. Then he turned to face the wall.

I Wonder ...
I wonder if you have ever told a lie because you were afraid . . .

[LORD], your kingdom is built on what is right and fair.

Psalm 89:14a

Worries

When the house was quiet, Matin got up and sat by the window. Streams of people marched toward the palace. He tried to imagine Anoush having fun, but his mind traveled to his first father—all the old bitter words. And to his first mother—all the old bitter glances of disgust when his leg was exposed.

At sundown, Matin heard noises and guessed that the banquet was over. Quickly he jumped back into bed.

"Matin," Anoush called, "I have a raisin cake for you."

Hunger pains from not eating all day urged him to take the cake. But with a heavy heart he pushed it away. "Save it for when I feel better," he said.

The next few days were worse instead of better.

Anoush and Carmeline talked about the banquet constantly, as if that was supposed to cheer him. Matin grew quieter. And he nibbled at his food.

One morning Matin climbed to the rooftop to be alone. But Gareb and Zenda were already there. He hid behind a basket of barley.

"I'm very worried," Zenda said. "Can't we find a doctor for Matin?"

Gareb's voice sounded far away. "It isn't a doctor he needs. Every day as I walk the fields, my mind isn't on the wheat. I only think of the hurt he buries inside of him."

Matin leaned back against the basket. He was a burden. It was time for him to leave. If Gareb couldn't do his work for the king, the whole family would be destroyed. Yes, for Anoush and Carmeline, he must leave.

I Wonder . . .
I wonder why it's so hard for Matin to trust people who love him . . .

Your truth and faithful love lead the way in front of you.

Psalm 89:14b

The King's Guest

Matin hobbled down the stone steps from the rooftop and down the streets of Jerusalem. The city gates were open. Merchants and people who worked the fields moved through the gates. There were so many people that he wouldn't be noticed.

But as Matin approached the gate, the guard reached out his arm. Then more guards appeared. They stopped the crowd, moved them to the side, and cleared a path.

The guard was so close to Matin he could smell the sweat on the leather breastplate. Had someone warned the guard? Were they looking for him?

Dust rose from the road that passed through the mountains. It was one of the king's chariots. Matin breathed a sigh of relief. As soon as the king's guest passed through, everything would be normal again.

The chariot moved slowly through the gate, so Matin had a chance to see the guest. The person of honor was a pale young man. He even looked a bit sickly.

"Who is that?" he asked the guard.

"Mephibosheth," the guard said. "His father was the king's best friend. He is also the grandson of the last king of our people. He is the only one left alive from that family. But he is lame, so King David wanted him to live here. Now King David will make sure Mephibosheth gets all he needs."

"Lame" echoed over and over in Matin's mind. How could this be? Was David really welcoming a lame person? What about Joab's threat?

I Wonder . . .
I wonder how you would answer Matin's questions . . .
Read the story of Mephibosheth in 2 Samuel 9:1-12.

[LORD], your arm is powerful. Your hand is strong.

Psalm 89:13

The Wrong Meaning

"**M**atin," called a voice. It was his father, Gareb. "Did you see Mephibosheth?"

Matin nodded. "Is he, I mean the Mephibosheth person—is he lame?"

Gareb put his arm around Matin. "Yes, somewhat like you. And that's okay, don't you think?"

"I'm afraid for him," Matin said. Then he told Gareb about what he overheard Joab say on the day Jerusalem was captured.

"Climb on my back," Gareb said. "You're not too big." With Matin on his back, Gareb took long strides up a grassy hill where there were rows of vines. A few grapes were ripe. Gareb picked them and gave them to Matin.

"What you heard Joab say had nothing to do with a person's body," he said, setting Matin down gently. "The kind of blind people David doesn't want in his kingdom are those whose eyes are blind to God. And the kind of lame people he doesn't want are those whose hearts are so wicked that it affects their whole body."

Matin tried to understand. "You mean David doesn't want anyone in his palace who doesn't love and honor God?"

"Exactly," Gareb said. "A body like yours has some problems, but nothing like the problems of a person who can't see God or trust in God with his heart."

Matin sobbed. He couldn't stop. Gareb held Matin tightly. "It's okay, my son. I love you. I see your heart opening to God. And because of God's blessing, there will not be a lame spot in your heart. There is a place of honor for you in God's kingdom."

I Wonder . . .
I wonder what "opening your heart to God" means . . .

Blessed are those who have learned to shout praise to you. LORD, they live in the light of your favor.

Psalm 89:15

Samuel Listens

1 Samuel 3

There is only one voice like yours. If you and thousands of other people record a sentence or two into an electronic voice reader, the voice reader can identify you when you speak to it again. Another person can come close to imitating the way you sound, but the electronic device can pick up the tiny differences.

God has a voice too. It isn't a voice you hear with your ears. It is one you hear with your heart. God's voice must not be confused with anything else that calls to you. You can know the message comes from God when it matches what God tells you in the Bible.

When Samuel first heard God calling, he didn't know it was God. He had to learn to recognize God's voice.

Psalm 85:8 tells you that if you listen, you will hear God's promises.

Litany	
Lambs	**Kids**
I will listen to what God the LORD will say.	
	He promises peace to his faithful people.

Song for the Week
"Be Still and Know," *Songs for LiFE* 225

Prayer for the Week
Lord, there are so many things to hear.
It is almost never quiet in my house or at school.
In all that noise, I forget to listen to you, Lord.
But when I listen, I hear great things.
Thank you for every promise you have spoken. Amen.

In a Sad, Dark Room

"Jamila. Jamila," a soft singing voice called from the courtyard.

Jamila slipped one finger between the window edge and the dark cloth that hung over the window. Through the tiny crack, she could see into the courtyard. That Israelite girl was out there with her lyre.

"Jamila." This time it was her sister, Meryl, calling. "Is someone here?"

"Shh," Jamila said, putting her finger over her lips. "It's the girl who plays the lyre. If we are very quiet, she won't know we're home."

"We should be friendly to her," Meryl said. "When I hear her music, it makes me forget about being sick."

Jamila moved away from the window. How could she explain to Meryl that the music was not for her. She was sure the Israelite girl was calling to get more people to play music in honor of the king or his God.

The rest of Jamila's family contributed to the new kingdom. Her brother, Tarik, honored the king at a banquet. Her father was a loyal stonecutter for the new building projects. And her mother devoted herself to producing purple weavings for the palace.

Wasn't that enough? All Jamila had the heart to do was take care of Meryl. Once she had prayed to the Israelite God about healing Meryl. But nothing happened.

Jamila unfolded a clean sleeping mat for Meryl. For the past week Meryl had been too weak to leave her bed.

"I'll roll you onto the new mat," Jamila said. "Then I'll bathe you with warm water."

I Wonder . . .

I wonder what you would tell Jamila if you could talk to her about God . . .

[God] is always there to help us in times of trouble.

Psalm 46:1b

Balsam Oil

Jamila eased Meryl onto the clean mat without any difficulty. But Meryl moaned when Jamila touched her with the warm bath cloths.

"What's wrong?" Jamila asked.

Meryl moved her hand to her left thigh. "It hurts to touch right there," she said, lifting her hand to expose red, oozing skin.

Sores! Jamila pulled back. Was she wrong when she told Mother no one could take better care of Meryl than a sister? Gently she dabbed the warm water around the spot. Soon, however, she discovered many small sores. Sores that would grow larger.

"Jamila," Meryl said faintly, "do you remember the soothing oil mother sometimes rubbed on us?"

The smell of the milky-yellow oil from the balsam berries rose in Jamila's memory. But it had been months since Mother had gone out to the Rephaim valley where the balsam trees grew. It wasn't safe in that valley because the Philistines gathered there when attacking Jerusalem. The Philistines didn't like David as the new king.

"Yes, the oil would take the sting out of your sores," Jamila said. "I'll check in Mother's jars." She was sure Mother didn't have a drop left, but there had to be some in the city somewhere. Or she could ask the gods to keep away the Philistines for the day. Then she could sneak out of the city, gather the balsam berries, and come back quickly.

The earth may fall apart. The mountains may fall into the middle of the sea. But we will not be afraid.

Psalm 46:2

I Wonder...

I wonder if you can remember a very scary time when you prayed to God for help...

Read the story of David and the Philistines in 2 Samuel 5:17-25.

The Rephaim Valley

The LORD who rules over all is with us.

Psalm 46:7a

A s soon as Meryl closed her eyes, Jamila left the room and climbed to the rooftop. Shielding out the sun, she looked to the southwest. It appeared quiet. Not a single Philistine showed his painted war face. Neither did any bronze shields reflect the sunlight.

Tarik had said that David overpowered the Philistines completely in the last battle. The Philistines were so badly frightened that they left behind precious, costly idols. Tarik had laughed, saying he didn't think those Philistines would come back so quickly. But then Tarik believed the story that God arranged for David to win the battle. Tarik tended to boast about God and the king. She'd ask her own gods to keep away the Philistines.

Jamila brushed her bangs off of her forehead and pinned them down. Even if she didn't understand what the Israelites believed, she wanted to look like one of them—at least while walking through the city. She peered around the courtyard wall before entering the street. A few children were playing games. If she moved normally among them to the city gate, no one would notice her.

Women who walked beside her turned the corners into their own court-yards. Small children scattered. But still she thought she heard footsteps—ones that slowed when she paused and hurried when she quickened her pace.

Once Jamila was outside the city gate, she ran without stopping. When she saw the tall balsam trees swaying in the breeze, she forgot all her troubles. She breathed in the rich fragrance before gathering the berries. Some of the berries were low enough, but the best ones were up high. She climbed the branches.

I Wonder . . .
I wonder what Jamila's gods looked like . . .
I wonder how she could believe they would protect her . . .

Up a Balsam Tree

Once Jamila climbed at least eight reeds high, she rested. Before collecting more berries, she gazed out beyond the branches. What she saw almost stopped her heart from beating. The valley was filling with Philistines. What happened to her prayer to the gods?

She looked up. There were plenty of branches hiding her from above. She looked to the sides. If she stayed close to the trunk of the tree, the fullness of the needles would cover her. Then she looked down. At the bottom of the tree stood the Israelite girl.

That explained the footsteps she had heard in Jerusalem. But even though this girl was a bother, she didn't deserve to be attacked by the enemy.

Branch by branch, Jamila lowered herself to the bottom limb. She held out her hand to the girl. "Get up here, quickly. The Philistines are surrounding us."

Jamila took the lyre while the girl hoisted herself up to the first branch. Jamila was tempted to touch the strings to see if music came out, but instead she returned it.

"Thanks for saving me," the girl said as they climbed to the middle branches. "It's a good thing you spotted them from up here."

"The gods must have been smiling on me," Jamila said.

The girl didn't say anything right away. Then she said, "There aren't any smiling gods. The Lord God is the one and only God."

"I have a hard time with your God," Jamila said. "I've asked your God to heal my sister. But she is getting worse."

A hollering bunch of Philistines clustered under their tree.

I Wonder . . .
I wonder why God doesn't always do what we ask him to do . . .

Come and see what the LORD has done.

Psalm 46:8a

Marching Treetops

Jamila shook so hard she was afraid she'd fall out of the tree.

The Israelite girl let go of the tree trunk. She steadied Jamila with her free hand. "We can whisper. The Philistines are too noisy to hear us." Then she pointed to a hill above the valley. "King David is out there with his men. They are surrounding the valley."

"But they're just standing there," Jamila said.

"They must be waiting for the Lord God," the girl said.

Jamila narrowed her eyes. "That's foolish."

"David waits for God," the girl said. "He listens to God. If we are still, we can listen too. The God who created this valley and this tree is all around us."

Jamila had never thought about God as a creator. But this tree was a gift. And gifts didn't come without givers.

Then marching sounds rose above them as if soldiers were in the treetops. Jamila was so frightened she thought she'd lose her grip. The girl squeezed her arm. "Don't be afraid. I think God is signaling David."

Hesitantly Jamila looked up. There were no soldiers above her—only branches. Then she looked down. The Philistines hadn't heard a thing. But David and his men had heard. They charged forward in one great moving force. The Philistines weren't prepared. In a short time they were struck down. And in the quiet after the battle Jamila said in awe, "The Lord is God."

"My name is Zarah," the girl said. "This has been quite an adventure. But I followed you to ask if music would help your sister."

Jamila touched Zarah's lyre. "Yes, the music of your God on your lyre." And she knew then that God had heard her first prayer. She just hadn't known that God was answering her prayer.

"Be still, and know that I am God."

Psalm 46:10a

I Wonder...

I wonder if you can remember some of the surprising ways God has answered your prayers...

The First King

1 Samuel 8-10

Think about something important you've been asked to do. Maybe you've been selected to carry the ring or the flowers in a wedding. The person who chose you thought you had special qualities that would help you do the job. After you were chosen, you were given things you needed for your job—special clothes, or a ring or flowers to carry.

God saw qualities in the young man Saul. So Saul became the first king of Israel. After Saul was chosen, the Bible tells us he was given gifts. First, his problem of the lost donkeys was taken care of. Second, he was given two loaves of bread from an offering. Finally, the Spirit of the Lord came upon Saul, giving him the heart he needed to be king.

Greater than being chosen for a number one job is being chosen as God's child. God gives you the gifts of the Spirit, listed in Galatians 5:22-23 (NIV).

Litany	
Lambs	**Kids**
But the fruit of the Spirit is	
	love
joy	
	peace
patience	
	kindness
goodness	
	faithfulness
gentleness	
	and self-control.

Song for the Week
"The Fruit of the Spirit," *Songs for LiFE* 188

Prayer for the Week
Lord, you call me to be your child.
Then you give me love, joy, peace, patience, kindness,
goodness, faithfulness, gentleness, and self-control.
With praise and thanks, I give you my heart. Amen.

Count the Good

Carmeline marked another line in the dirt and added up forty-nine lines. It was her job to count every bundle of wheat carried to the threshing floor.

Counting was only one of the harvesttime jobs. It wasn't the job she wanted, but it was the one Father chose for her.

Matin struggled up the hill with his wheat bundle.

"You're carrying a giant's load," she shouted. "Keep up the good work."

She waved with both hands at the next man and his donkey. "Two hands for two bundles," she called to him.

"Your cheerfulness is contagious," he said.

Before she finished counting the lines again, Matin appeared beside her. "Guess what!" he said. "Father has a new job for me. I'm working with the wind. Watch."

She waited until he reached the high point of the threshing floor. Then she signaled that she saw him. He tossed the grain into the air just as a breeze stirred. The wind blew away the light chaff, and the grain tumbled to the ground.

As golden clouds surrounded Matin, Carmeline wished Father had a new job for her. One that was more important than drawing stick lines.

Anoush, Carmeline's eight-year-old adopted sister, came skipping over. She had a new doll made out of wheat stalks. "Father says he wants to see you. My doll and I can do the counting."

I Wonder . . .
I wonder if it is possible to enjoy a job when it isn't your favorite thing to do . . .

Trust in the LORD and do good. Then you will live in the land and enjoy its food.

Psalm 37:3

The Watch Girl

Carmeline kissed Anoush on the head and ran to the top of the threshing floor. As the breeze lifted her hair and freedom pounded through her feet, she wondered what kind of job Father had in mind.

Father stood in the center of the circular floor, surrounded by bundles of wheat.

"Father," she called. "Anoush is doing the counting."

He pushed back his head scarf. "I have an important job that requires a person who is alert, honest, and kind. I've watched you all morning. I've seen your desire to do your best at a simple job. Your attitude tells me I can trust you to do more."

Excitement rose in Carmeline's chest. "What is it?"

Father combed the chaff out of his beard. "The wife of my watchman is about to give birth to her first child. He wants to be with her. But the harvest is so abundant I can't give up my other workers to take over for him. What do you think about being the watch person?"

Carmeline imagined herself sitting high in the tower watching over all the fields.

"You'd have to take the donkey, Malak," Father said. "If there is an emergency, he'll go fast for you. And if a thief comes, alert my field men. They'll handle it."

She bit her lip. The job was more challenging than she had expected. But Father chose her and trusted her. He had recognized what was in her heart. "Yes, Father," she said. "I won't let you down. I'll do it."

I Wonder . . .

I wonder how you feel when someone trusts you to do good . . .

Find your delight in the LORD. Then he will give you everything your heart really wants.

Psalm 37:4

Alert and Honest

Commit your life to the LORD. He will make your godly ways shine like the dawn.

Psalm 37:5a, 6a

Carmeline climbed the steps to the watchtower. She viewed the fields in every direction. Whole families were living in the fields until the harvest was over.

There were so many people and so many stalks of grain, she feared the job was too great for her. Without closing her eyes, she looked to the mountains beyond the fields and asked for God's protection. And for the ability to do the job Father expected.

In the far corner of the field a small child sat alone. She appeared to be crying. Hezro cut grain with his sickle directly below the watchtower.

"Hezro," she called, "go to the far northeast corner of the field. I think a child is in trouble. If you can't help her, bring her back here."

Before Hezro returned, a mother climbed the watchtower steps. "I've lost my daughter. May I search the fields from up here?"

"She's coming now." Carmeline pointed to Hezro carrying the girl in his arms.

"Bless you," the mother said. "You have the eyes of an eagle."

As mother and daughter reunited, Carmeline knew Father would be pleased.

Another kind of cry got her attention next. A man below the tower shook his fist.

"Where's the watchman?" he asked. "I don't feel safe with you in the tower."

"I'm a bit afraid myself," Carmeline said. "I was only chosen because more important people had other work to do."

The man's dark eyes met Carmeline's. "At least you're honest. I'll spread the word for all to keep watch in our small sections. Then I can work to provide for my family."

I Wonder . . .

I wonder if being honest is something that's important to you . . .

A Mistake?

Carmeline drank half the water from her deerskin bag. She never thought watching could make someone so thirsty. The sun moved slowly across the sky.

Stay awake, she told herself. She jumped in place. She splashed water on her face. It helped a bit. Thinking about how she had proved herself to be alert and honest helped too. But what about kindness? If she rested in the shady side for a small measure of time, she'd at least be showing kindness to herself.

No, that wasn't what Father meant. She walked slowly around the inside edges of the tower. Workers moved from the fields to their tents, escaping the afternoon heat.

A few poor people moved into the fields, picking up grain that had dropped to the ground. A woman in dirty, ragged clothing attracted Carmeline's attention. The woman picked a few kernels, then she stretched and looked around. Carmeline decided this was a chance to show kindness. She left the watchtower, leaping over cut stalks until she met up with the harsh and wild-looking woman.

Carmeline worked beside the woman, filling a bag of grain for her. "This is for you," she said to the woman.

The woman's eyes flashed angrily. "You owe me more grain than I can carry. But there are two children in your city who can carry the grain for me. Matin and Anoush."

Carmeline felt her entire body go weak. This must be Matin's and Anoush's mother. How could she offer kindness to a wicked mother?

I Wonder . . .

I wonder if Carmeline should show kindness to someone who doesn't deserve it . . .

The power of those who are evil will be broken. But the LORD takes good care of those who do what is right.

Psalm 37:17

Kindness?

"**M**atin and Anoush," Carmeline said, giving herself time before answering.

"They're probably slaves in a household in Jerusalem," the woman said.

A tricky answer popped into Carmeline's head. "I don't know any slaves by those names." It was true. The only Matin and Anoush she knew were her brother and sister.

The woman shrugged. "Give me more grain, or I'll search the city for my children."

Carmeline loaded Malak with heavy grain bags, surprising herself at her own strength. She presented the donkey to the woman.

Without a thank you or a farewell glance, the woman mounted the donkey. She slapped the donkey until it moved under her command. Carmeline pictured Malak dumping off his passenger. At first she liked that picture, but perhaps this woman still had some love left for Matin and Anoush.

"Wait," Carmeline called. "It's a fast donkey. But if you beat it, it'll dump you."

The woman didn't heed Carmeline's call. She slapped the donkey again.

When Father checked on Carmeline a short time later, she told him the story of her confusion over kindness.

"You offered kindness with self-control," Father said. "It sounds as if she came for the food, not her children. God will judge what is evil."

At sundown, Malak returned. He had no rider. Only the bags of grain were on his back. Carmeline set out these grain bags for the poor.

At the feast of firstfruits, Carmeline offered to God the first loaves of bread baked from the new wheat. She thanked God for the golden grain of harvest and for the gift of self-control that helped keep Matin and Anoush in her family.

I Wonder . . .

I wonder if you've ever asked God for the gift of kindness . . . or the gift of self-control . . .

Be still. Be patient.
Wait for the
LORD to act.

Psalm 37:7a

Saul Disobeys

1 Samuel 15

Do you remember the last time your parents punished you for something? Did you have to give up your allowance? Time with your friends? One of your favorite activities?

In this week's Bible story, Saul was punished for disobeying God. Because he had disobeyed, no more kings would come from his family. He lost closeness with God. Happiness never filled Saul's life again.

None of us are able to obey perfectly all of the time. Sometimes we disobey our parents. And often we disobey God. We deserve to be punished.

But there is someone who obeyed God perfectly—all of the time. That someone is Jesus Christ. And he made it possible for you to be forgiven for all the times you disobey too! This week think about the wonderful gift of forgiveness that Jesus bought for you by dying on a cross. Repeat Jesus' words from John 14:6.

Litany	
Lambs	**Kids**
Jesus answered,	
	"I am the way
and the truth	
	and the life."

Song for the Week
"Believe in the Lord," *Songs for LiFE* 223

Prayer for the Week
Lord, the only way to you is through Jesus.
Thank you for forgiveness through your Son, my Savior.
I rejoice in Jesus who is the way, the truth, and the life. Amen.

Read the biblical account of David's first attempt to bring the ark into Jerusalem in 2 Samuel 6:1-9.

Who Can Hear Jehesah?

Does he who made the ear not hear?

Psalm 94:9a

Jehesah carried his harp to the rooftop. He ducked under the white linen garments hanging out to dry. All throughout Jerusalem, the Levites played music. They tuned their harps and lyres or worked on rhythms with their cymbals and tambourines.

Tomorrow there would be a grand procession. The king and all the people were marching to Kiriath-Jearim. The ark of the Lord was there. In a great ceremony, they would carry the ark to Jerusalem. David had pitched a special tent for the ark.

In the streets and in the market everyone told a story about the ark. Some said the Philistines had taken it long ago, but it caused sickness and death among their people so they sent it to Kiriath-Jearim. Some said if you even climbed the hill to where the ark was hidden, you would die. David said the ark belonged in Jerusalem because it was named after the Lord, who rules over all. He wanted everyone in Jerusalem to worship the Lord.

Jehesah tightened the third sheep-gut string on his harp. The seventh and twelfth strings were too tight, so he lengthened them. Going from the shortest string to the longest, he plucked each one. Yes, each string made the right sound. He strummed his fingers across the harp to play a song. It sounded like dull thumps. Why didn't he have the same spirit of music as his father, who crafted the best harps in Jerusalem?

Lately Jehesah hid his sour notes by only pretending to play. He'd stand next to a harpist whose sounds floated by sweetly. Then without touching the strings, he acted as if he were strumming. But the fearful stories of the ark scared him. If God was present in the ark, would God notice that Jehesah, the son of a Levite, couldn't play one sweet note?

I Wonder . . .
I wonder what you should do when you don't want God to hear something you do or say . . .

A New Harp

Jehesah heard laughing voices lift from the street below. He walked to the rooftop edge. His sister, Zarah, played her lyre. Ronia, Abbie, Carmeline, Matin, Anoush, Jory, and Elias were all following her. They all thought Zarah was a great lyre player. It was going to Zarah's head. She said her music brought joy. And just the other day she bragged about how the sick girl, Meryl, grew stronger hearing her music.

Jehesah was the oldest son of Heman. People should be saying good things about his music. He hated being passed up by his sister. He worked harder on his music than she did. Yet she had it all—music and friends.

A rumbling of wooden wheels against stone distracted him from watching Zarah and the others. It was the ox-cart man, pulling a new ox-cart toward the palace. King David must have ordered it for moving the ark.

It made sense that only a new cart would be good enough for the ark. Could a new harp be the answer to his problem with music? He hung his harp on a clothesline pole, leaving the wind to play it.

In his father's shop two new balsam-wood harps were ready to play. He was about to take one when he noticed a golden cypress-wood harp. The strings had not been attached yet, but otherwise it was identical to the king's. Long strips of drying sheep gut hung from the ceiling, waiting to be used. I'll finish this harp, he thought. I'll have a harp the same as the king's, and then I'll play as sweetly as the king. He'd stay out of Father's sight during the procession tomorrow. Then Father would never know.

I Wonder . . .
I wonder what you should do when you don't want God to see something you're doing . . .

Does he who formed the eye not see?

Psalm 94:9b

—233—

Tight Strings

Jehesah stroked the wood on the harp. It was smooth and glossy. He loved the scent of new wood rubbed with oil.

Yes, he had to have this harp. Perhaps this kind of wood improved the sound. Father probably had not attached the strings yet because he had too much music to prepare. He didn't have any time to work in the shop the last few days.

Jehesah placed two benches on top of each other and climbed on top so he could reach the ceiling. Then he dropped all the sheep guts off the ceiling hooks. When he hopped down, all the guts were in a pile. He had seen Father arrange the guts in order of length, but there wasn't time to do that. The top gut in the pile fit the length in the middle of the harp. One gut at a time, he tied the bottom knots and then wrapped them on the pegs at the top. He was finished. It was a work of art. His finger were damp and sweaty. But tomorrow he'd have on a white robe and clean hands. Yes, tomorrow he'd make sweet music.

At the evening meal Jehesah was as excited as everyone else over the upcoming day. But it was hard to sleep that night. He tossed from side to side, trying to picture himself playing sweet music. Instead, flashes of broken sheep guts interrupted his dream.

In the morning, Jehesah ran to the shop. The harp was even more beautiful in the morning light. And the strings were tight. His dreams had caused him to worry for nothing.

Already the streets were filled with music. There wasn't time to practice. He hurried outside. Hundreds of harp players surrounded his home.

I Wonder . . .
I wonder if this harp is going to work for Jehesah . . .

LORD , blessed is the man you correct.

Psalm 94:12

The Ark of an Awesome God

In a short time Jehesah was swallowed into the mass of musicians. Several men complimented him on the beauty of his harp. Soon he forgot that he had taken it without permission. He held his head proudly.

None of the musicians played their instruments on the six-mile walk to Kiriath-Jearim. But there was plenty of rejoicing and storytelling. The old people who traveled from far away surprised Jehesah the most. Many rode donkeys or carts, but one old woman who had a cloud of white hair had walked every step. She must have been at least ninety years old. She was so ancient, she remembered the ark from when she was a girl.

Jehesah gazed into the bright gleam in her eyes as he listened to her story.

"When I was a young girl, the ark was kept in a special tabernacle in Shiloh. We always knew God was with our people when the ark was there. My heart beat a faster rhythm whenever we went up to meet our great and awesome God."

As the great parade of people climbed the hill near Kiriath-Jearim, Jehesah's heart pounded. He climbed a rock just off the path. It gave him a better view above the heads of the thousands in the parade.

King David and the priests stood near the entrance of a house. Then, with precise steps, two men came out carrying a golden box. Two golden figures with wings sat on top of the shimmering box. Not a sound rose from the crowd of thousands.

The silence made Jehesah uneasy. He stepped off the rock. Again the woman was beside him. "Did you see it?" she asked. "The throne of God . . . between the cherubim?"

I Wonder . . .
I wonder if you can think of a time when *you* felt God's majesty . . .

The LORD rules. He puts on majesty as if it were clothes.

Psalm 93:1

Thumping Strings and Stumbling Oxen

"Who are those men?" Jehesah asked, pointing to the men lifting the ark on the cart.

"Uzzah and Ahio," the old woman said, "the grandsons of Abinadab, the man who stored the ark when it came back from the Philistines. But something isn't right."

Jehesah pressed his cypress wood harp against his chest. What did the old woman sense was not right? The rejoicing began. Everything seemed exactly right.

As the procession neared a threshing floor just outside of Jerusalem, David danced with all his might. His face glistened with moisture. The harps, lyres, tambourines, and cymbals kept rhythm with David. Jehesah hadn't played yet. He squirmed to the front of the procession right next to the ark. *Now,* he said to himself. With a great strike he hit the strings. The worst thudding sound he had ever heard thumped out of the harp.

Shocked, he looked around to see if anyone had noticed. The dancers hadn't stopped. Neither had the musicians. One of the oxen stumbled though. Uzzah reached over to steady the ark so it wouldn't fall off the cart.

Then before Jehesah could blink, Uzzah fell to the ground. The procession stopped. One of the priests knelt beside Uzzah. "He's dead!" the priest cried.

Then people started running. Many screamed that God was angry at them for bringing out the ark. Jehesah couldn't move. Had his horrible notes caused the oxen to stumble? But why was Uzzah killed for preventing the ark from falling?

Jehesah knew he had to return the harp to Father's workshop and keep his awful music a secret.

I Wonder . . .

I wonder if there are things about God that Jehesah doesn't understand . . .

I wonder if there are things about God that you don't understand . . .

[The LORD] . . . will again judge people in keeping with what is right.

Psalm 94:15a

Samuel Anoints David

1 Samuel 16

W here will you hear music this week? Will it be on the radio, in a movie, in your school, or in a game you play? Music may relax you or lift your feet to dance. It can carry words to your heart.

But music must be in tune to do wonderful things.

A heart that doesn't know God or obey God is without a melody. King David was in tune with God. The psalms that he wrote reflect a right heart.

I wonder where your heart is as you finish this book. Praise God this week with Psalm 98:1, 4-6. May your heart be in tune with God all your life.

Litany	
Lambs	**Kids**
Sing a new song to the LORD .	
	He has done wonderful things.
Shout to the LORD with joy.	
	Make music to the LORD with the harp
Shout to the LORD with joy.	
	He is the King.

Song for the Week
"Hallelujah, Praise the LORD," *Songs for LiFE* 24

Prayer for the Week
I will honor you, my God and King.
I will praise your name for ever and ever.
Every day I will praise you.
I will praise your name for ever and ever. Amen. (Psalm 145:1-2)

Read the biblical account of David bringing the ark into Jerusalem in 2 Samuel 6:9-19 and 1 Chronicles 15:1-29.

Questions

J ehesah considered throwing the harp behind the trees. Maybe that would get rid of the awful feeling in his heart and stomach. Then he remembered the words of the old woman, "Something isn't right." She was wise. If he had caused the oxen to stumble, she'd tell him. Finding out the truth had to be better than this frightening wondering. Or would it?

He ran from group to group, but no one had seen a woman with a cloud of white hair and eyes that gleamed like oiled wood. Neither had anyone seen an old woman of any description traveling by herself. Was she only a dream? A dream that announced something was wrong before it happened?

Slowly Jehesah continued his way back to Jerusalem. By now people had stopped running, but their talk ran from one idea to another. All of them were wondering how to explain the death of Uzzah.

Some blamed Uzzah, saying he didn't have enough respect for God. Others blamed David for attempting to move the ark at all.

A priest said David was afraid of God now because of God's anger against Uzzah.

Jehesah kept walking as if in a trance. He had no direction in mind; he was simply following the people in front of him. His only thought was that he'd be better off if the mountains fell down upon him. Better off covered with stone than living with this guilt.

People bumped into him as they pressed to pass through the city gates. So Jehesah didn't realize Father was beside him until Father called Jehesah's name.

"I've been looking for you," Father said, "hoping you survived all the confusion."

Jehesah sensed Father's gaze dropping down to the harp. "My new harp!" Father said. "How is it that you have it?"

Jehesah's head fell in shame.

I Wonder...

I wonder how you feel when someone discovers that you did something wrong . . .

God, see what is in my heart. Know what is there.

Psalm 139:23a

A Wood-chip Boy

Father's hand was heavy on Jehesah's shoulder. In the crowd of people Father was silent. Jehesah knew Father's rebuke would come when they were alone in the workshop.

Once inside the workshop, Father crossed his arms over his chest.

Jehesah had no choice but to begin the long, ugly story.

In the awful silence after Jehesah finished speaking, Father removed the strings from the cypress wood harp. "The guts weren't ready," he finally said. "They must be rolled and formed into thick and thin strings. You've seen me do that before."

Jehesah closed his eyes. Yes, that was right. He hadn't been thinking.

Father continued. "Concerning the death of Uzzah, no one knows for sure. I heard some say the oxen stumbled over the bordering stones of the threshing floor. All that I'm sure of is that Uzzah went against the Lord."

It was scary to think about God's anger. Jehesah undid the pegs as Father untied the knotted guts.

Father stood. "You also must consider your ways," he said to Jehesah. "How are you not right with the Lord? You can do your thinking while you sweep out the shop."

After sweeping in every corner, Jehesah carried wood chips and dust outside. I'm nothing more than a wood-chip boy, he thought. That made him remember Ronia and how she had called herself the raisin girl. After she gave him the invitation to the palace banquet, he never went back to see her. With all his worries there hadn't been time to think of anyone except himself.

I Wonder . . .
I wonder if God ever shows you what isn't right in your life . . .

[God], see if there's anything in my life you don't like.

Psalm 139:24a

A Cry in the Wind

Jehesah heard a cry. It sounded as if it came from the rooftop of his house. He ran up the stone steps. No one was there. His harp hung from the pole where he had left it the other day. It was almost as if the crying sound came from the harp, so he reached for it. He heard the cry again. This time he looked down below where a bent figure sat in the street. With his harp, he ran back down to the street.

An old beggar woman raised her cup. "Water," she said. "From the stream that makes the city of God glad."

If she had asked for a simple cup of water from a jug, Jehesah might have done it. But he wasn't going all the way to the Gihon. He walked away from her.

But the cry came back. This time he thought he heard his name in the cry. Returning to the beggar, he took her cup and gave her his harp to hold. He ran through the streets, out the city gate, and down the steps to the spring. It was silly to go all that way for just one cup, but now that he had, he returned with the water. The old woman took it, but didn't drink it. Instead she handed him the harp.

"Play for me," she said.

"I can't. My heart is empty of music."

"You have spoken the truth," she said. "Your heart is empty of music because it is empty of love for God and others. The Spirit of God can't live in a selfish heart. Ask for forgiveness." Her sad eyes reflected a slight gleam—one of polished wood.

Then he knew she was the old woman from the procession.

I Wonder . . .

I wonder what the woman meant when she said that God's Spirit can't live in a selfish heart . . .

Help me live in the way that is always right.

Psalm 139:24b

A New Song from a New Heart

Jehesah bowed his head. The old woman was right about his heart. His music had always been for himself. It had never been for God or for others. Not like Zarah, whose music was always a gift. "Forgive me, Lord," he prayed.

When he lifted his head, the woman was drinking the water.

"God's blessings are like a river," she said. "They fill the city of God with joy."*

"Your words sound like music," he said.

"Play the music you hear in my words," she said.

He touched the strings. Then he put the harp down. "I'm afraid."

"The king is afraid too," the woman said. "He is afraid to bring the ark into Jerusalem. But soon he'll see that God is good. And so will you. Goodbye, Jehesah. May God bless you."

"Wait," he called. But she was gone before he could say thank you. Without thinking, he plucked a "thank you" on the harp. It sounded right. He plucked it again. Another "thank you" came to him. This time it was for God. He played eight more notes.

The mountains and hills around Jerusalem glowed under the late afternoon sun. The olive trees were in bloom, and the fruit trees had knobs of new fruit. Jehesah balanced his harp on a stone and played a song of praise to God for creation. Before long a crowd gathered around him. All together they praised God for gifts of life and beauty.

Then Jehesah sang, "God's blessings are like a river. They fill the city of God with joy."

I Wonder . . .

I wonder what makes you sing a song of thanks to God . . .

*Psalm 46:4a

I heard a sound from heaven. It was like the roar of rushing waters and loud thunder. The sound I heard was like the music of harps being played. Then everyone sang a new song in front of the throne. . . . They had been set free from the evil of the earth.

Revelation 14:2-3

In the Presence of God

Three months later, Jehesah learned that David had again made plans for the ark. Jehesah decided to work on a new crutch for Matin instead of joining the procession.

Zarah came into the shop. "Sapphira is on the rooftop, waiting to see you."

Israelites from miles around were in Jerusalem, but who was Sapphira? How did this person know him? When he reached the rooftop, he saw the old woman. "Sapphira?"

Her smiled crinkled her entire face. "Has God given you streams of blessings?"

This time it was Jehesah's turn to smile as he played his harp for her.

"The king is carrying the ark into Jerusalem according to God's commands to Moses long ago," Sapphira said. "The priests are ready. It will be carried on poles, not on a man-made oxcart." She stretched out her hand to Jehesah. "You must get dressed in your white linen."

"My music is too simple," he said.

"Even a small praise from the heart is pleasing to God," Sapphira told him. Then she left.

But Jehesah heard her wisdom and understood it. He dressed in his white robe.

When the ark came out in all of its golden glory, Jehesah thought his heart would burst. God was present! Jehesah's fingers strummed against the strings. "Sing a new song to the LORD. He has done wonderful things" (Ps. 98:1). Jehesah felt his small song enlarge into a grand, joyous song as thousands joined him. The sun shone brightly in the deep blue sky. There was only one white cloud, reminding him of Sapphira. The next time he saw her, he'd thank her for teaching him the secret of the harp. Now he understood that he must love God above all and love others as much as himself.

I Wonder . . .
I wonder if you understand the secret Jehesah learned from Sapphira . . .

"May praise and honor for ever and ever be given to the One who sits on the throne and to the Lamb! Give them glory and power for ever and ever!"

Revelation 5:13b

Words, Places, People, and Things to Know

Abinadab A man who lived in Kiriath-Jearim. The ark of God was brought to his house because the Philistines were afraid to keep it.

Ahio In the Bible he is mentioned as the son of Abinadab. But Ahio was most likely a grandson of Abinidab. The ark was at his place until King David came for it.

alabaster This is a natural material that is easily carved. Often precious ointments were stored in jars made from alabaster. It has a light color.

altar The altar was important in Old Testament worship. It was the place where offerings or sacrifices were made to God for the forgiveness of sins. The blood of the animal on the altar showed that life—the greatest gift from God—had to be given as the price for sin. Today we don't have altars in our worship. Jesus is our sacrifice to God.

anoint To apply oil on a person. It was done to dedicate a person to God.

ark of the covenant A wooden box covered with gold inside and outside. Rings of gold were on each corner of the ark. Poles covered with gold were made to go through these rings. Two winged cherubim (angels) covered the top. Inside Moses placed the two stone tablets with the commandments from God.

When the Philistines destroyed the tabernacle at Shiloh, they took the ark. Even though it came back to Israel, the ark was not in a place dedicated to God until David brought it to Jerusalem.

The ark represented God's presence with the people. Today God is with us through the Holy Spirit, who lives in us.

Ashdod One of the five major cities of the Philistines. Ashdod was their center of worship for the god Dagon. The ark of God was brought to this city.

Baal Baal was the name for the main god of the Canaanites.

balsam oil Oil made from the bark, leaves, and berries of the balsam tree. The pale-yellow gum from the tree was dissolved in water to make the ointment. It was used as a medicine. Sometimes this oil was called balm.

balsam tree A bushy evergreen tree. It grew twelve to fourteen feet high.

Bethel A town twelve miles north of Jerusalem. One of the towns Samuel visited on a regular basis after the people returned to the Lord.

blessing The father of a family blessed his children and grandchildren. The blessing promised certain things would come true for the person blessed. When we ask God to bless us, we are asking for God to see and meet our needs. When we say blessings to God, we come to God with praise and worship.

booth This is a shelter built of tree branches with the leaves left on. It served as a home away from home—like a camping tent—when the Israelites celebrated the fall harvest and remembered their wanderings in the desert.

bronze A metal made from copper and tin and used for pots and mirrors. Some shields were also made from bronze.

Canaanite The people who lived in the promised land when the Israelites first came. At that time the land was called Canaan.

cherubim They are heavenly creatures—angels. They were represented on the ark of the covenant as winged creatures with human-animal forms with the faces of lion, ox, man, and eagle.

cistern A place dug into the earth or rock for collecting rainwater or spring-water. Some cisterns were very deep. They were covered—usually with a stone lid. Sometimes other things, including people, were put into cisterns.

City of Refuge Moses and Joshua set aside certain cities as cities of refuge. The roads to these cities were always kept clear. A person accused of a crime was protected in these cities until a judge could decide whether or not the person was guilty.

clay jar A jar made from soil and water. It was formed and hardened in the sun or in an oven.

copper A heavy reddish-gold metal found near the surface of the ground. It was found in the land of Canaan—the promised land.

cypress wood Wood from the cypress tree. It was a hard, strong wood.

Dagon The god of the Philistines. He may have been pictured with the upper body of a man and the lower body of a fish. Dagon is also referred to as a grain god.

digit The width of a finger. Three-fourths of an inch.

Ephraim The younger son of Joseph. In the promised land divisions were made among the twelve tribes, coming from the twelve sons of Jacob. But actually the land was divided into thirteen sections, because Joseph's section was divided between his two sons—Manasseh and Ephraim. The land of Ephraim had good soil and plenty of rainfall. Shiloh, the place where Joshua set up the tabernacle, was in the land of Ephraim. So the blessing Jacob gave Ephraim, the younger son, seems to have come true in this land. But Psalm 78 says the blessing was taken away from Ephraim and given to the tribe of Judah.

King David came from the tribe of Judah. And from this tribe, God promised the Messiah.

flint knife Flint is a dull, gray stone. It was used for arrowheads, spear points, and knives.

gazelle A swift-running antelope.

Gibeon A city northwest of Jerusalem and southwest of Mizpah.

Gihon Spring A spring just outside of Jerusalem on the east side. The name *Gihon* means "gushing." At one time the water may have gushed up from the spring, cutting through the rock. At the time of the Jebusites, when David captured Jerusalem, there were most likely natural tunnels and shafts leading from the spring to places under the city. Later, King Hezekiah dug a more accessible tunnel.

Gilgal A town northeast of Jerusalem. Gilgal is the place where the Israelites crossed the Jordan River and entered the promised land with Joshua. It is one of the towns Samuel visited.

goatskin bag Bottles used for water and milk were made from the skin of animals.

granary A building to store things such as grain, armor, food, or jewels.

harps The harps of the Bible were played with the fingers. They had twelve strings. King David is the most famous biblical harp player. His harp most likely was made of cypress wood. When King Solomon built the temple, he had all the harps and the supports of the temple made from almugwood. (See Kings 10:12; almugwood may have been sandalwood.)

The harp strings were made of sheep gut cut into long strips, then dried and rolled. The guts were passed through a form with different sized holes to produce thicker or thinner strings. They were attached by pegs at the top and knots in the inside bottom.

King David most likely used his harp while writing psalms.

No one really knows how David's harp music sounded. But the sound of the harp was never pleasing to God when the player did not have a heart that was right with God (see Isaiah 5:12 and Amos 5:23).

Hebron A place where Abraham lived, and the site of David's first palace.

homer A measurement equal to about sixty gallons.

iron A metal that is formed through a heat process. When the Israelites came into the promised land, the Philistines operated all of the ovens for producing iron. So until David had the Philistines under control, it was difficult for the Israelites to obtain iron.

Jebusites A tribe of Canaanites. They lived in Jerusalem for a long time before David captured the city.

Kiriath-Jearim The town west of Jerusalem where the ark of God was stored after the Philistines returned it.

leather sheath A protective jacket for a knife.

Levites The tribe of God's people coming from Jacob's third son, Levi. At Mount Sinai, Moses assigned this tribe a special place in worship. The priests and musicians were Levites.

lime A white lumpy powder that, when mixed with water, can dissolve certain things.

lyre A musical instrument with ten strings. It was played using a bone chip or wood chip.

measuring reed A measuring length that is about 105 inches long.

metal box on door frames Every Israelite door had a tube-shaped metal or wooden box on the doorpost. It was called a *mezuzah*. Inside the box were the words from Deuteronomy 6:4-9. Often before a Jew entered or left home, he would kiss his fingers and place them on the *mezuzah*. It was a sign of faith in God and a reminder of God's words.

millstone A millstone is actually made of two stones. One fits inside of the other. The smaller one moves over the grain or olives in the larger stone. The grain is then crushed into flour.

minas A measuring weight. It is about 1.1 pounds.

Mizpah A town north of Jerusalem. It was one of the towns Samuel visited. When this town was uncovered by archeologists, many four-room houses were found. And small furnaces were found outside the town.

myrrh It was sold as a spice, medicine, or cosmetic. Women sometimes attached bags of myrrh to their clothing for fragrance.

oil lamp Small clay, dish-like containers. A wick (small cord of woven fibers) soaked up the oil and gave fuel for the light.

olive oil Most of the oil used in Bible times came from pressed olives. It was pressed in a mill where the upper stone rolled over the olives on the lower stone. The oil was used for cooking, anointing, and lighting.

papyrus A plantlike reed that grew along the Nile River in Egypt. So much paper was made from this reed that paper was often called papyrus.

Philistines These people entered Canaan mostly from the Mediterranean Sea. They controlled five cities, ruled by lords, along the coast. The Philistines often fought against the Israelites.

plumb line This tool was used to measure whether a wall was straight. It had a small cone connected to a cord with a wood piece at the other end. The wood piece was placed at the top of the wall. If the wall was straight, the cone at the end would barely touch the wall at the bottom.

priest One who was dedicated to serving God in religious or holy matters.

Ramah A town north of Jerusalem. Samuel's parents came from this town. And Samuel went back there to live when the tabernacle at Shiloh was destroyed.

scales When trades were made that depended on weight, a balance was used. Each side of the scales had a tray or dish. On one side weights (usually stones of a certain standard weight) were used. On the other side was placed the silver, gold, or other object.

scapegoat The second of two goats used on the day when sins were paid for. The first goat was sacrificed as a sin offering, but the priest laid his hands on this second goat (scapegoat), saying it carried the people's sins. Then the goat was sent out into the wilderness as a sign to the people that their sins were gone. They never had to worry about these sins again.

scroll A scroll or roll of paper was the usual form of a book in Bible times. Several sheets of papyrus paper were glued together. It was then rolled on rods. The beginning of the scroll was on the right and the end on the left. The people wrote from right to left.

Shechem One of the cities Joshua assigned as a City of Refuge.

shekel A weight measurement, about .4 ounces. It was often used in the weighing of precious metals such as gold and silver. Later it became the worth of a coin.

Shiloh The place where the tabernacle was set up when the Israelites settled in the promised land. Shiloh was never rebuilt after the Philistines destroyed it during the time of Samuel.

tabernacle The tent-like structure that Moses constructed under God's command. The Israelites worshiped God in this tabernacle in the wilderness and in Shiloh. The tabernacle stood for God living with the people.

tambourines This musical instrument was a small drum made of a wooden hoop and probably two skins. It was played to keep rhythm.

threshing floor The place where the grain was separated from the plant during harvest. The bundles of grain were spread on the smooth, packed earth. Then oxen pulling heavy wooden sleds trampled over the grain. Usually the threshing floors were on high flat places so that they were open to the wind. The wind blew away the chaff (the useless covering on the seed of the grain).

tooth-edged hammer A tool used by a stonemason (one who shaped stones for building).

Uzzah The grandson of Abinadab. He touched the ark of the Lord and died because of it.

watchtower Shelters were built in the fields so that the crops could be guarded during harvest. During this time a guard occupied the tower throughout the day and the night.

white linen garments White clothing stood for purity, cleanliness, and joy. On special worship days or days of gladness and joy, the priests and Levites wore white linen.

Yes and No stones It is only a guess that these objects were stones. Yes and No stones were carried by the priests and were used something like we use dice. The way that they landed somehow revealed God's will.

Calendar

Activities/Special Days	Stories Relating to Special Days
September-October Plowing *Feast of Trumpets* The New Year celebration	Week 2: "Creation: Owls and Octopuses, Panthers and People" Week 3: "Creation: Taking Care of God's World"
The Day When Sins Are Paid For (Atonement) Confession and forgiveness for sins	Week 5: "Cain and Abel"
Feast of Booths Five days after atonement. It marked the completion of the harvest. Time of joy and remembering the wanderings in the desert.	Week 6: "Rain and Rainbows"
October-November Grain planting	
December-January Spring growth	
January-February Winter figs	
February-March Pulling flax Almonds bloom	
March-April Barley harvest *Passover* (or Feast of unleavened bread). Celebrated freedom from slavery in Egypt.	Week 27: "The Fall of Jericho"

Activities/Special Days	Stories Relating to Special Days
April-May	
General harvest	
May-June	Week 34: "The First King"
Wheat harvest	
Vine tending	
Pentecost (also called Day of the Firstfruits or Feast of Harvests). Marks the end of wheat harvest. Offerings were given of the firstfruits of harvest.	
June-July	
First grapes	

The Ten Commandments

God gave ten commandments to Moses on the mountain. They are written in Exodus 20:1-17.

Many of the stories in *Rooftop* have something from the commandments in them. What can you find about the commandments in each of these stories?

1. Do not put any other gods in place of me.

   Week 4: "Sin Spoils God's World"
   Week 7: "The Tallest Tower"
   Week 12: "God Blesses Jacob"
   Week 19: "The Ten Plagues"

2. Do not make statues of gods that look like anything in the sky or on the earth or in the waters. Do not bow down to them. I, the LORD your God, am a jealous God.

   Week 4: "Sin Spoils God's World"
   Week 16: "Joseph the Governor"

3. Do not misuse the name of the LORD your God. The LORD will find guilty anyone who misuses his name.

4. Remember to keep the Sabbath day holy. Do all of your work in six days. But the seventh day is a Sabbath in honor of the LORD your God. Do not work on that day. The same command applies to your sons and daughters, your male and female servants, and your animals. It also applies to any outsiders who live in your cities. In six days I made the heavens and the earth. I made the oceans and everything in them.

   Week 2: "Creation: Owls and Octopuses, Panthers and People"
   Week 11: "Jacob Steals the Blessing"
   Week 12: "God Blesses Jacob"

But I rested on the seventh day.
So I blessed the Sabbath day
and made it holy.

5. Honor your father and mother.
Then you will live a long time in
the land the LORD your God is
giving you.

6. Do not commit murder.

7. Do not commit adultery.

8. Do not steal.

9. Do not give false witness against
your neighbor.

10. Do not long for anything that
belongs to your neighbor. Do not
long for your neighbor's house,
wife, male or female servant, ox
or donkey.

Week 13: "Jacob Meets Esau"
Week 18: "The Burning Bush"
Week 19: "The Ten Plagues"
Week 26: "Crossing the Jordan"

Week 18: "The Burning Bush"
Week 30: "Samson"
Week 21: "Manna and Quail"

Week 17: "The Birth of Moses"
Week 21: "Manna and Quail"
Week 28: "Deborah and Jael"

Week 5: "Cain and Abel"
Week 11: "Jacob Steals the
            Blessing"